CW01672451

In S

of

Souls

New England
in
the Eighteenth Century

JONATHAN EDWARDS

&

DAVID BRAINERD

J.R.Broome

2002

GOSPEL STANDARD TRUST PUBLICATIONS
12(b) Roundwood Lane, Harpenden, Herts.
AL5 3DD, England.

© J.R.Broome 2002

ISBN: 1 897837 36 4

Published by:
Gospel Standard Trust Publications

Cover picture: Autumn Scene, River Jackson,
New Hampshire, U.S.A.

Printed and bound in Great Britain by
The Cromwell Press
Aintree Avenue, White Horse Business Park,
Trowbridge, Wiltshire. BA14 0XB

Contents

Chapter **Page**

PREFACE

When the Pilgrim Fathers left Leyden in the Netherlands for America in July 1620, William Bradford, their chronicler, records that one of their motives in moving across the Atlantic was to be the means of propagating the gospel among the heathen. Another of their desires was that the Lord would open the eyes of the Jews to the Messiah, take away the veil from their eyes and graft them into the natural olive tree. [2 Corinthians 12. 14-16. Romans 11.24].

Both Jonathan Edwards and David Brainerd were direct descendants of the Pilgrim Fathers and were used of the Lord as instruments in His hand in the outpouring of the Spirit in revival power in New England in the early eighteenth century. Northampton, where Edwards was minister from 1729 - 1750, was the scene of great revival in 1735 and 1741. These events were recorded in Jonathan Edwards' books *A Narrative of Surprising Conversions* published in 1736 and *The Distinguishing Marks of a Work of the Spirit of God* published in 1741.

The effects of these blessings in New England were felt in England, in the home country, at the same time. David Brainerd, who eventually was led among the Indians, witnessed revival under his own ministry in 1745. This is recorded in his *Life and Diary* published after his death in 1747 by his friend Jonathan Edwards.

In this way the prayer of the Pilgrim Fathers was answered. The heathen were blessed; even Jonathan Edwards himself, when forced to give up his pastorate at Northampton, went to Stockbridge, an out post to the west, and preached among the Indians. Similarly, as the United States has stood by present-day Israel, we wait to see the second answer to the prayer of the Pilgrim Fathers, in the outpouring of the Spirit on Israel.

CHAPTER 1

JONATHAN EDWARDS
(1703 - 1758)

A New Life Given

Birth and Childhood

Jonathan Edwards was born on 5th October 1703 at Windsor, New England, on the banks of the River Connecticut. His ancestors were exiles from England in the great Puritan exodus. His father was minister at Windsor for about sixty years. He died in 1758 at the age of eighty-nine only two months before his son Jonathan. Jonathan's parents had married in 1694 and lived in partnership for over sixty-three years. His mother was Esther Stoddard, daughter of Solomon Stoddard, minister of Northampton, the place where, in later years, Jonathan himself became minister. His mother lived to be ninety. She had ten daughters and one son. Four were older than Jonathan and six younger.

Jonathan was educated with care. He had godly parents and it was their desire that from a child he might know the Holy Scriptures. He was a sober and quiet boy, yet a strong and highly intelligent character.

The blessing which attended his father's ministry did not pass him unnoticed. His earliest extant letter is written to one of his sisters away from home, dated Windsor 10th May 1716. He writes, "Through the wonderful mercy and goodness of God there hath been in this place a very remarkable stirring and pouring out of the Spirit of God, and likewise now is, but I think I have reason to think it is in some measure diminished but I hope not much. About thirteen have been joined to the Church in a state of full communion… I think there come commonly on Mondays about thirty persons to speak with father about the condition of their souls. It is a time of general health in this place."

The loving concern of Mr. Edwards for his family is seen in a letter he wrote home, while a military chaplain in 1711. He wrote to his wife, "Remember my love to each of the children, to Esther, Elizabeth, Anne, Mary, Jonathan, Eunice, and Abigail. The Lord have mercy on and eternally save them all, with our dear little Jerusha. The Lord bind up their souls with thine and mine in the bundle of life. Tell the children, that I would have them, if they desire to see their father again, to pray daily for me in secret; and above all things to seek the favour of God in Christ Jesus, and that while they are young".

Adolescence

In his youth Jonathan was the subject of various religious impressions, especially as a result of the blessing which visibly rested on his father's ministry at Windsor. About twenty years later he wrote of how the Lord had worked in his heart in the years from about 1713 to 1723. In those years he was at home under his father's tuition until he entered Yale College at New Haven in 1716, where he studied for six years. He was licensed to preach the gospel at the age of nineteen and went to his first church in New York in August 1722, where he stayed for eight months and then returned to Windsor at the end of April 1723. In September 1723 he went to Yale to receive his M.A. and stayed there studying and preaching occasionally until June 1724 when he was made a tutor at the college. It is to this period of his life that the following account of the Lord's dealings with him belongs. As many regard him as a divine in America of comparable stature to John Owen in England, it is of interest to know that his knowledge of the truth was through the revealing of the Holy Spirit.

His Own Account of his Conversion

He writes, "I had a variety of concerns and exercises about my soul from my childhood; but I had two most remarkable seasons of awakening, before I met with that change by which I was brought to those new dispositions, and that new sense of things, that I have since had. The first time was when I was a boy, some years before I went to college, at a time of awakening in my father's congregation. I was then very much affected for many months and concerned about my soul's salvation, and was abundant in religious duties. I used to pray five times a day in secret and to spend much time in religious conversation with other boys, and used to meet with them to pray together … I with some of my school mates joined together and built a booth in a swamp, in a very retired spot for a place of prayer. And besides I had particular places of my own in the woods, where I used to retire by myself, and was from time to time much affected … I seemed to be much in my element when engaged in religious duties. I am ready to think many are deceived with such affections and such a kind of delight as I then had in religion, and mistake it for grace.

But in progress of time my convictions and affections wore off and I entirely lost all these affections and delights and left off secret prayer, at least as to any constant preference for it, and returned like a dog to his vomit, and went on in the ways of sin. Indeed I was at times very uneasy, especially towards the latter part of my time at College, when it pleased God to seize me with pleurisy; in which He brought me nigh to the grave and shook me over the pit of hell. And yet it was not long after my recovery before I fell again into my old ways of sin. But God would not suffer me to go on with any quietness. I had great and violent inward struggles, till after many conflicts with wicked inclinations, repeated resolutions and bonds, that I laid myself under by vows to God, I was brought wholly to break off all former wicked ways and all ways of known outward sin, and to apply myself to seek salvation and practise many religious duties, but without that kind of affection and delight I had formerly experienced.

My concern now wrought more by inward struggles and conflicts and self reflection. I made seeking my salvation the main business of my life. But yet it seems to me, I sought it after a miserable manner, which has made me sometimes since question whether ever it issued in that which was saving, being ready to doubt whether such miserable seeking ever succeeded. I was indeed brought to seek salvation in a manner that I never was before; I felt a spirit to part with all things in the world for an interest in Christ. My concern continued and prevailed with many exercises, thoughts and inward struggles, but it yet never seemed to be proper to express that concern by the name of terror.

From my childhood my mind had been full of objections against the doctrine of God's sovereignty in choosing whom He would to eternal life, and rejecting whom He pleased, leaving them eternally to perish and be everlastingly tormented in hell. It used to appear like a horrible doctrine to me. But I remember the time very well, when I seemed to be convinced and fully satisfied as to this sovereignty of God, but I never could give an account how or by what means I was thus convinced, not in the least imagining at the time, nor a long time after, that there was any extraordinary influence of God's Spirit in it. However my mind rested in it and it put an end to all those cavils and objections. There has been a wonderful change in my mind with respect to this doctrine from that day to this…

But I have often since that first conviction had quite another sense of God's sovereignty. I have often had since not only a conviction but a delightful conviction. Absolute sovereignty is what I love to ascribe to God. The first instance that I remember of that sort of inward, sweet delight in God and divine things, that I have much lived in since was on reading those words, 1 Timothy 1.17, 'Now unto the King eternal, immortal, invisible, the only wise God, be honour and glory for ever and ever. Amen'. As I read those words, there came into my soul a sense of the glory of God. … Never any words of Scripture seemed to me as these words did. … How happy should I be, I thought, if I might enjoy that God and be rapt up in Him in Heaven and be as it were swallowed up in Him for ever. I kept saying those words of Scripture to myself and prayed in a manner quite different from what I used to do, with a new sort of affection. But it never came into my thought, that there was anything spiritual or of a saving nature in this.

Christ Revealed in his Heart

From about this time I began to have a new kind of apprehensions and ideas of Christ and the work of redemption and the glorious way of salvation by Him. An inward sweet sense of these things at times came into my heart, and my soul was led away in pleasant views and contemplations of them. My mind was greatly engaged to spend my time in reading and meditating on Christ, on the beauty and excellency of His person and the way of salvation by free grace in Him. Those words in the Song of Solomon 2. l. used to be abundantly with me, 'I am the rose of Sharon and the lily of the valleys.' The words seemed to me to represent the loveliness and beauty of Christ. The whole book of the Canticles used to be pleasant to me and I used to read it much.

His Account of it to his Father

Not long after I first began to experience these things I gave an account to my father of some of the things that had passed in my mind. I was pretty much affected by the discourse we had together; and when the discourse was ended, I walked abroad alone in a solitary place in my father's pasture for contemplation. And as I walked there and looking upon the sky and clouds, there came into my mind so sweet a sense of the glorious majesty and grace of God, as I know not how to express; I seemed to see them both in sweet conjunction; majesty and meekness joined together; it was a sweet, and gentle, and holy majesty; and also a majestic meekness, an awful sweetness; a high, and great, and holy gentleness.

New York

My sense of divine things seemed gradually to increase till I went to preach at New York, which was about a year and a half after they began, and while I was there I felt them very sensibly in a much higher degree than I had done before. My longings after God and holiness were much increased. Pure and humble, holy and heavenly, Christianity appeared to me exceedingly amiable. I felt a burning desire to be, in everything, a complete Christian, and conformed to the blessed image of Christ, and that I might live, in all things, according to the pure, sweet and blessed rules of the gospel. I had an eager thirsting after progress in these things; which put me upon pursuing and pressing after them.

It was my continual strife, day and night, and constant inquiry, how I should be more holy, and more becoming a child of God and a disciple of Christ. I now sought an increase of grace and holiness, with much more earnestness than ever I had sought grace before I had it … but yet with too great a dependence on my own strength; which afterwards proved a great damage to me. My experience had not then taught me, as it has done since, my extreme feebleness and impotence, every manner of way, and the bottomless depths of secret corruption and deceit there was in my heart. However, I went on with my eager pursuit after more holiness and conformity to Christ. …

There was no part of creature-holiness that I had so great a sense of its loveliness, as humility of heart and poverty of spirit; and there was nothing that I so earnestly longed for. My heart panted after this - to lie low before God, as in the dust, that I might be nothing, and that God might be all, that I might become as a little child. I had the abundance of sweet religious conversation in the family where I lived, with Mr John Smith and his pious mother. My heart was knit in affection to those in whom was the appearance of true piety; and I could bear the thought of no other companions, but the disciples of the blessed Jesus. I had great longings for the advancement of Christ's kingdom in the world; and my secret prayers used to be in great part taken up in praying for it. …

I frequently used to retire into a solitary place, on the banks of the River Hudson, at some distance from the city, for contemplation on divine things and secret converse with God and had many sweet hours there. Sometimes Mr Smith and I walked there together, to converse on the things of God and our conversation used to turn much on the advancement of Christ's kingdom in the world, and the glorious things that God would accomplish for His church in the latter days. I had then, and at other times, the greatest delight in the Holy Scriptures of any book whatsoever. Oftentimes in reading it every word seemed to touch my heart. I felt a harmony between something in my heart, and those sweet and powerful words. I often seemed to see so much light exhibited by every sentence, and such a refreshing food communicated, that I could not get along in reading, often dwelling long on one sentence, to see the wonders contained in it. Almost every sentence seemed to be full of wonders.

Returns Home to Windsor

I came away from New York in the month of April 1723 and had a most bitter parting with Mrs Smith and her son. My heart seemed to sink within me at leaving the family and city, where I had enjoyed so many sweet and pleasant days. I went from New York to Wethersfield by water; and as I sailed away I kept sight of the city as long as I could. However, that night after this sorrowful parting I was greatly comforted in God at West Chester, where we went ashore to lodge, and had a pleasant time of it all the way to Saybrook. It was sweet to me to think of meeting dear Christians in heaven, where we should never part more. At Saybrook we went ashore to lodge on Saturday and there kept the Sabbath, where I had a refreshing season walking alone in the fields.

After I came home to Windsor I remained much in a like frame of mind as when at New York, only sometimes I felt my heart ready to sink with the thoughts of my friends at New York. My support was in contemplations on the heavenly state. It was a comfort to think of that state where there is fullness of joy, where there reigns heavenly calm and delightful love without alloy, where there are continually the dearest expressions of this love, where is the enjoyment of the persons loved, without ever parting. And how will the mutual lovers join together to sing the praises of God and the Lamb. How will it fill us with joy to think that this enjoyment, these sweet exercises will never cease, but will last to all eternity."

Here Jonathan Edwards' account of the Lord's work in his soul ends. In it can be seen how he was struggling in his own strength to be holy, and also how as he looked back on it when he wrote much later in his life, he understood his youthful ignorance of his own weakness and the plague of his own heart. Nevertheless as it stands it shows clearly the Lord's beginning with him.

CHAPTER 2

Early Years

Early Resolutions

Besides the writings already quoted, Jonathan Edwards left two other documents relating to his early years. One is a set of resolutions written between the years of his college days and the end of 1723, and the other a *Diary* written mainly in the years 1722-1725.

There are seventy resolutions in all and they begin with the words, "Being sensible that I am unable to do anything without God's help, I do humbly entreat Him, by His grace, to enable me to keep these resolutions, so far as they are agreeable to His will, for Christ's sake." While there is no scriptural warrant for making such resolutions and there appears to be a certain legality about many of them, yet there is about them much that is good.

"*Resolved*, to act in all respects, both speaking and doing, as if nobody had been so vile as I and as if I had committed the same sins, or had the same infirmities or failings as others; and I will let the knowledge of their failings promote nothing but shame in myself, and prove otherwise."

"*Resolved*, never to do anything out of revenge."

"*Resolved*, never to speak evil of anyone, so that it shall tend to his dishonour, more or less, upon no account except for some real good."

"*Resolved*, in narrations, never to speak anything but the pure and simple truth."

"*Resolved*, never to allow the least measure of any fretting or uneasiness at my father or mother."

"*Resolved*, after afflictions, to inquire what I am the better for them; what good I have got by them." It would seem that in his youthful zeal his desires were good, while he later learnt much of his own weakness and inability to keep these resolutions.

In his *Diary* these resolutions come in for comment, which is of interest. For **Wed., Jan 2nd 1722**, he wrote, "Dull. I find by experience, that let me make resolutions, and do what I will, with never so many inventions, it is all nothing, and to no purpose at all, without the motions of the Spirit of God; for if the Spirit of God should be as much withdrawn from me always, as for the past week, notwithstanding all I do, I should not grow but should languish and miserably fade away. I perceive, if God should withdraw his Spirit a little more, I should not hesitate to break my resolutions and should soon arrive at my old state. There is no dependence on myself. Our resolutions may be at the highest one day, and yet, the next day, we may be in a miserable dead condition, not at all like the same person who resolved. So that it is to no purpose to resolve, except we depend on the grace of God. For if it were not for His mere grace, one might be a very good man one day, and a very wicked one the next.

I find also by experience that there is no guessing out the ends of Providence, in particular dispensations towards me - any otherwise than as afflictions come as corrections for sin, and God intends when we meet with them, to desire us to look back on our ways, and see wherein we have done amiss, and lament that particular sin, and all our sin before him - knowing this also that all things shall work together for our good, not knowing in what way, indeed, but trusting in God."

His *Diary* December 1722 - June 1725

The *Diary*, to which we have referred begins in December 1722 and ends, except for a few entries, in June 1725. It covers most of his time in New York, a period of five months at his home at Windsor, April-Sept. 1723, and a period of study at Yale College beginning in Sept. 1723, until he was appointed a tutor in June 1724. He stayed at Yale, until he became co-pastor of the church at Northampton in February 1727, at the age of twenty-three, assisting his grandfather, Mr Stoddard. The *Diary* therefore covers the period of his life between the ages of nineteen until twenty-two. It shows how he sought to lead a holy life and miserably failed in all his efforts, only to be brought to a realisation that he could do nothing without the Lord's help, which it took him many lessons to learn fully. It was never intended for publication and was kept by him to be a reminder of his own weakness and the Lord's goodness.

On **January 10th 1723** he wrote, "It is a great dishonour to Christ, in whom I hope I have an interest, to be uneasy at my worldly state and condition; or when I see prosperity in others and all things go easy with them, the world is smooth to them, and they are very happy in many respects, and very prosperous, or are advanced much in honour; to grudge them their prosperity, or envy them on account of it, or to be in the least uneasy at it, to wish and to long for the same, and to desire that it should be ever so with me. Wherefore concluded always to rejoice in every one's prosperity, and not to pretend to expect or desire it for myself; and to expect no happiness of that nature as long as I live; but to depend on afflictions, and to betake myself entirely to another happiness."

On **January 12th** in considering the subject of mortification of the deeds of the body (Romans 8.13.) he wrote, "It is suggested to me that too constant a mortification and too vigorous application to religion, may be prejudicial to health." This type of seeking the Lord bears some resemblance to Luther in his monastery at Erfurt.

But it is interesting by **January 15th** to find him writing, "Alas! how soon do I decay. O how weak, how infirm, how unable to do anything of myself! What a poor inconsistent being! What a miserable wretch without the assistance of the Spirit of God! While I stand, I am ready to think that I stand by my own strength, and upon my own legs; and I am ready to triumph over my spiritual enemies, as if it were I myself that caused them to flee: when alas! I am but a poor infant, upheld by Jesus Christ, who holds me up, and gives me the liberty to smile to see my enemies flee, when he drives them before me. And so I laugh, as though I myself did it, when it is only Jesus Christ leads me along, and fights Himself against my enemies. And now the Lord has a little left me, how weak do I find myself! O let it teach me to depend less on myself to be more humble, and to give more of the praise of my ability to Jesus Christ! The heart of man is deceitful above all things and desperately wicked; who can know it?"

It is clear from other entries in the *Diary* that follow about this time, that the lesson regarding his own impotency was one he found very hard to learn and that he needed much teaching to bring him to Toplady's experience,

> Nothing in my hand I bring,
> Simply to Thy cross I cling;
> Naked, come to Thee for dress;
> Helpless, fly to Thee for grace;
> Foul, I to the Fountain fly,
> Wash me, Saviour, or I die.

On March 2nd 1723 he wrote, "O how much

pleasanter is humility than pride! O that God would fill me with exceeding great humility, and that He would evermore keep me from all pride! The pleasures of humility are really the most refined, inward and exquisite delights in the world. How hateful is a proud man! How hateful is a worm that lifts up itself with pride! What a foolish, silly, miserable, blind, deceived worm am I, when pride works."

On **Saturday, April 7th** he was in a low place and wrote, "This week I found myself so far gone, that it seemed to me I should never recover more. Let God of His mercy return to me, and no more leave me thus to sink and decay! I know, O Lord, that without Thy help I shall fall innumerable times, notwithstanding all my resolutions, how often soever repeated."

In **May 1723** the Lord granted him a sight of the great value of godly parents and he sweetly writes, "I now plainly perceive, what great obligations I am under to love and honour my parents. I have great reason to believe; that their counsel and education have been my making; though in the time of it, it seemed to do me so little good. I have good reason to hope, that their prayers for me have been, in many things, very powerful and prevalent, that God has, in many things, taken me under his care and guidance, provision and direction, in answer to their prayers for me. I was never made so sensible of it as now." When Jonathan Edwards wrote this he was living at home after some months in New York. It is a great mercy when we are brought to such a sense of gratitude in the lifetime of our parents, though often such a realisation comes after they are taken.

Besides such considerations as parental indebtedness, young Edwards thought about his end and wrote **July 5th 1723**, “Last night, when thinking what I should wish I had done, that I had not done, if I was then to die; I thought I should wish, that I had been more importunate with God to fit me for death, and lead me into all truth, and that I might not be deceived about the state of my soul.”

Regarding that state of his soul he wrote on **August 12th** “The chief thing that now makes me in any measure to question my good estate, is my not having experienced conversion in those particular steps, wherein the people of New England and formerly the dissenters of Old England, used to experience it. Wherefore, now resolved, never to leave searching, till I have satisfyingly found out the very bottom and foundation, the real reason, why they used to be converted in those steps.” His own beginning had been gradual, like Nicodemus, and he was looking at the cases of those whose beginnings had been marked, like the Apostle Paul, with a sudden deep conviction of sin. It would have been a blessing if the result of his search was to show him that the Lord is sovereign in how he works in the souls of each of his dear people.

Yale College September 1723

In September 1723 Jonathan left home and went to Yale College at New Haven to study and receive his degree of Master of Arts. His *Diary* for the following year contains such remarks as, "Who can understand his errors? O that I might be kept from secret faults!" Regarding a tendency to exaggeration he writes, "I must be contented where I have anything strange or remarkable to tell, not to make it appear so remarkable as it is indeed, lest through fear of this, and the desire of making a thing appear very remarkable I should exceed the bounds of simple truth."

Tutor at Yale June 1724

When he was appointed a tutor at Yale, he wrote on **June 6th 1724** in his *Diary*, "This week has been a very remarkable week with me, with respect to despondencies, fears, perplexities, multitudes of cares and distraction of mind; it being the week I came hither to New Haven in order to entrance upon the office of tutor of the College. I have now abundant reason to be convinced of the troublesomeness and vexation of the world, and that it will never be another kind of world." He was leaving the quiet world of his studies and entering upon his life's work of teaching and preaching. Life, he was already finding, was a battle. Speaking of this period in his writings he says, "I continued much in the same frame in the general as when at New York, till I went to New Haven as tutor of the College. … After I went to New Haven, I sunk in religion, my mind being diverted from my eager pursuits after holiness, by some affairs that greatly perplexed and distracted my thoughts.

Taken Ill at New Haven

In September 1725, I was taken ill at New Haven, and while endeavouring to go home to Windsor, was so ill at the North Village, that I could go no further; where I lay sick for about a quarter of a year. In this sickness God was pleased to visit me again with the sweet influences of his Spirit. My mind was greatly engaged there in divine and pleasant contemplations and longings of soul. I observed that those who watched with me would often be looking out wishfully for the morning; which brought to my mind those words of the Psalmist, and which my soul with delight made its own language, 'My soul waiteth for the Lord, more than they that watch for the morning; I say, more than they that watch for the morning.' When the light of day came in at the window, it refreshed my soul from one morning to another. It seemed to be some image of the light of God's glory. I remember, about that time, I used greatly to long for the conversion of some that I was concerned with. … But some time after this I was again diverted with some temporal matters, that exceedingly took up my thoughts, greatly to the wounding of my soul, and went on, through various exercises, that it would be tedious to relate, which gave me much more experience of my own heart than I had before."

CHAPTER 3

In Search of Souls

Assistant Minister at Northampton

On the 15th February 1727, Jonathan Edwards was ordained minister of the gospel, and placed over the church at Northampton as an assistant to his grandfather Mr Stoddard. He was 23 years of age. His grandfather was then in his eighty-fourth year, and had been minister at Northampton for fifty-five years. He was a faithful minister and highly respected in the town. But one circumstance relating to the church at Northampton was to be a cause of considerable sorrow to Jonathan Edwards in years to come. During the early history of the church, from the time of its formation and during the life of Mr Mather, the minister, and for upwards of thirty years after the settlement of Mr Stoddard, the church practised strict communion. Some time after 1704 Mr Stoddard opened the table. It is noteworthy that the strict communion practised before 1704 "admitted none to the Lord's Supper, except those who, after due examination, were regarded in the judgment of the church as regenerate persons". At the settlement of Jonathan Edwards in 1727 the lax situation had been in operation for twenty-two years and, there is no doubt, must have had a bad effect on the church. Jonathan Edwards had some hesitation about the matter when he first came to Northampton, but did not become fully convinced regarding strict communion until some years later, and did not publicly reveal his mind on the subject until the spring of 1749, the result being that the church at Northampton forced him to resign his pastorate, as a majority disagreed with him. Thus the seeds of trouble existed in the church in 1727 which were to be the cause of his having to leave his pastorate.

His practice was to preach on Sundays and in the week, to encourage his people to come to his home to see him, but only to visit them when they were sick or under some special affliction. He also spent a large part of his time writing and published a number of books on various subjects. He often spent at least twelve hours a day in his study and had remarkable powers of self-discipline. He usually rose about four or five in the morning and allowed himself a period of relaxation with his family in the evening. His only other relaxation was riding on horseback, walking, and in winter, rather like William Gladstone, the 19th century British Prime Minister, he would take an axe and fell a tree or chop wood.

His marriage and Pastorate at Northampton

In the same year as he commenced his pastorate (1727), on the 28th July, he married Sarah Pierrepont.

She was at the time eighteen years old. She was a godly young woman and became a good pastor's wife. His aged grandfather Mr Stoddard died on February 11th 1729, and Jonathan Edwards was then sole pastor at Northampton. Nothing unusual attended his life and ministry until 1734. At that time a violent controversy prevailed in his part of New England concerning Free Will, which caused him to preach a number of sermons on the doctrine of justification by faith alone. For this he was ridiculed by many, both at Northampton and elsewhere. But in his own congregation the Lord blessed these sermons. In the latter part of December five or six people were remarkably converted, in such a way as to cause notice among the majority of the inhabitants of Northampton.

Revival at Northampton 1735

His biographer says, "The year 1735 opened in Northampton in a most auspicious manner. A deep and solemn interest in the great truths of religion had become universal in all parts of the town, and among all classes of people. This was the only subject of conversation in every company; and almost the only business of the people appeared to be, to secure their salvation. So extensive was the influence of the Spirit of God, that there was scarcely an individual in the town, either old or young, who was left unconcerned about the things of eternity. … 'The town', says Jonathan Edwards, 'was never so full of love, nor so full of joy, nor yet so full of distress, as it was then.'

Whenever he met the people in the sanctuary, he not only saw the house crowded, but every hearer earnest to receive the truth of God, and often the whole assembly dissolved in tears, some weeping for sorrow, others for joy, and others from compassion.

In the months of March and April, when the work of God was carried on with the greatest power, he supposed the number of genuine conversions to have been at least nearly thirty a week. During the winter and spring, many persons from the neighbouring towns came to Northampton, to attend his ministry. Having heard contradictory reports of the state of things, they came to see and examine for themselves. Of these, numbers had their consciences awakened, were savingly wrought upon, and went home rejoicing in the forgiving love of God. The sermons which were most used were those he preached from Romans chapter 3 verse 19, 'That every mouth may be stopped,' in which he showed that God will be just if He cast every sinner into eternal condemnation."

The Revival Declines

By the end of May 1735 the revival began to lessen. Excitement of a natural kind, emotion and controversy, all the work of the enemy, as is so often the case in times of revival, began to appear. Also, it is quite clear that, as on the day of Pentecost, the outpouring of the Holy Spirit was given at a particular time and in a particular place. Jonathan Edwards was to witness another such outpouring later, when George Whitefield visited America and came to preach for him at Northampton in 1740. Then both of those godly ministers were able to converse on the Lord's work at Northampton in 1735, both having experienced remarkable revival attending their labours in the gospel, Whitefield in England and Edwards in America.

His Own Soul's Experience 1729 -1739

Regarding his own soul's experience in the first ten years of his ministry Edwards wrote, "Since I came to Northampton, I have often had sweet complacency in God, in views of His glorious perfections, and of the excellency of Jesus Christ. God has appeared to me a glorious and lovely Being, chiefly on account of His holiness. The holiness of God has always appeared to me the most lovely of all His attributes. The doctrines of God's absolute sovereignty, and free grace, in showing mercy to whom He would show mercy, and man's absolute dependence on the operations of God's Holy Spirit, have so often appeared to me as sweet and glorious doctrines. These doctrines have been much my delight. God's sovereignty has ever appeared to me a great part of His glory. It has often been my delight to approach God, and adore Him as a sovereign God, and ask sovereign mercy of Him.

It has often appeared to me delightful, to be united to Christ; to have Him for my Head, and to be a member of His body; also to have Christ for my Teacher and Prophet. I very often think with longings and pantings of soul, of being a little child, taking hold of Christ, to be led by Him through the wilderness of this world. That text Matthew 18.3. has often been sweet to me, 'Except ye be converted, and become as little children' etc., I love to think of coming to Christ, to receive salvation of Him, poor in spirit, and quite empty of self, humbly exalting Him alone; cut off entirely from my own root, in order to grow into and out of Christ; to have God in Christ to be all in all; and to live, by faith on the Son of God, a life of humble, unfeigned confidence in Him.

That Scripture has often been sweet to me. Psalm 115:1. 'Not unto us, O Lord, not unto us, but unto Thy name give glory, for Thy mercy, and for Thy truth's sake.' And those words of Christ Luke 10:21. 'In that hour Jesus rejoiced in spirit, and said, I thank thee, O Father, Lord of heaven and earth, that Thou hast hid these things from the wise and prudent, and hast revealed them unto babes: even so, Father, for so it seemed good in Thy sight.' That sovereignty of God, which Christ rejoiced in, seemed to me worthy of such joy; and that rejoicing to show the excellency of Christ, and of what spirit He was. …

Revelation of Christ to his soul 1737

Once, as I rode out into the woods for my health, in 1737, having alighted from my horse in a retired place, as my manner commonly has been, to walk for divine contemplation and prayer, I had a view, that for me was extraordinary, of the glory of the Son of God, as

Mediator between God and man, and His wonderful, great, full, pure, and sweet grace and love, and meek and gentle condescension. This grace that appeared so calm and sweet, appeared ineffably great with an excellency enough to swallow up all thought and conception - which continued, as near as I can judge - about an hour … which kept me the greater part of the time in a flood of tears. … And I have had on occasions an affecting sense of the excellency of the Word of God as a word of life; as the light of life, a life-giving word; accompanied with a thirsting after that word, that it might dwell richly in my heart.

I have had views of my own sinfulness and vileness very frequently, to such a degree as to hold me weeping, sometimes for a considerable time together; so that I have often been forced to shut myself up. I have had a vastly greater sense of my own wickedness than ever I had before my conversion. It has often appeared to me, that if God should mark iniquity against me, I should appear among the worst of mankind... Very often, for these many years these expressions are on my mind and in my mouth, 'Infinite, upon infinite! … I have greatly longed of late for a broken heart, and to lie low before God. …

Knowledge of Sin and Salvation

It is affecting to think how ignorant I was when a young man of the depths of wickedness, pride, and deceit left in my heart. I have a much greater sense of my complete dependence on God's grace and strength, and His sole good pleasure than I had formerly; and have experienced more abhorrence of my own righteousness … though still afflicted with a proud and self-righteous spirit. I see the serpent putting forth its head everywhere around me, though it seems to me I was a far better Christian for the two years after my conversion than I am now, and lived in a more earnest sense of the absolute sovereignty of God, with a delight in that sovereignty and the glory of Christ, as the Mediator revealed in the gospel.

One Saturday night in particular, I had such a discovery of the excellency of the gospel that I could but say to myself, 'This is my chosen light, my chosen doctrine'; and of Christ, 'This is my chosen prophet'. It was sweet beyond all expression to follow Christ and to be taught, enlightened, and instructed by Him; to learn of Him, and live to Him.

Another Saturday night (Jan. 1739) I had a sense how sweet and how blessed a thing it was to walk in the way of duty; to do that which was right and meet to be done, agreeable to the holy mind of God … I could not but cry out, 'How happy are they who do that which is right in His sight! They are blessed indeed, they are the happy ones.' I had, at the same time, a very affecting sense of how meet and how suitable it was that God should govern and order all things according to His own pleasure, and in this I rejoiced."

Here the personal narrative of Jonathan Edwards ends.

Revival in New England 1740

Before the second revival began at Northampton in 1740 there had been a great blessing felt in the preaching of the gospel in England, Wales and Scotland under the preaching of such men as George Whitefield, Howell Harris and Daniel Rowlands. When in 1740 George Whitefield visited the American colonies of Georgia and South Carolina, he was invited by ministers at Boston to come to New England. Here in September he preached to large congregations and there was evidence of great blessing attending his ministry.

George Whitefield at Northampton 1740

On leaving Boston he went to Northampton where he arrived on October 17th. He records in his *Journal* how he came to preach in Jonathan Edwards' pulpit and says, "When I came into his pulpit I found my heart drawn out to talk of scarce anything besides the consolations and privileges of saints, and the plentiful effusion of the Spirit upon the hearts of believers. And when I came to remind them of their former experiences, and how zealous and lively they were at that time (the revival at Northampton in 1734-5), both minister and people wept much." On Sunday, October 19th, Whitefield preached and records, "Preached this morning and good Mr. Edwards wept during the whole time of exercise. The people were equally affected and in the afternoon the power increased yet more. Our Lord seemed to keep the good wine to the last. Oh!

that Northampton people may recover their first love and return and do their first works."

Edwards' Account of These Events

Writing to a neighbouring minister in December 1743 Edwards gives a very full account of the revival which followed Whitefield's visit and the blessing which continued during the following two years. He says, "Ever since the great work of God that was wrought here nine years ago (1734) there has been a great and abiding alteration in this town. … And though after that great work there has been a very lamentable decay of religious affections … yet there are some few instances of awakening and deep concern about the things of another world even in the most dead time. In the year 1740 in the spring before Mr. Whitefield came to this town, there was a visible alteration; there was more seriousness especially among young people … it was a very frequent thing for persons to consult their minister upon the salvation of their souls. …

Mr Whitefield's sermons were suitable to the circumstances of the town, containing a just reproof of backslidings, and in a most moving and affecting manner making use of our great professions and great mercies, as arguments with us, to return to God from whom we had departed. Immediately after this the people appeared more engaged in religion … to meet frequently and embrace all opportunities to hear the preached word. The revival appeared at first chiefly among professors … to whom Mr. Whitefield addressed himself … but in a very short time there appeared an awakening and deep concern among some young persons, that looked upon themselves as in a Christless state; and there were some hopeful appearances of conversion and some professors were greatly revived. In about a month or six weeks there was a great attention in the town, both as to the revival of professors and the awakening of others. By the middle of December a considerable work appeared among those that were very young.

In the month of May (1741) a sermon was preached (by Jonathan Edwards) to a company at a private house. Near the conclusion of the discourse one or two persons that were professors were so greatly affected with a sense of the greatness and glory of divine things and the importance of the things of eternity, that they were not able to conceal it ... many others at the same time, especially among the young, were overcome with distress about their sinful condition, so that the room was filled with nothing but outcries, faintings and the like. Others soon heard of it in several parts of the town and came to them, and what they saw and heard there was greatly affecting to them.

There seemed to be a consequent happy effect of that meeting to several particular persons. After it were meetings, from time to time, attended with like appearances."

Jonathan Edwards in this letter goes on to explain that some of the work bore fruit but some bore no fruit to perfection and proved to be but natural emotions, things which appeared for a season and then vanished away. He continues, "Others were deeply impressed, their convictions took fast hold of them and abode by them; and there were some that from one meeting to another seemed extraordinarily affected for some time, but to little purpose, their affections presently vanishing from time to time; but yet afterwards were seized with abiding convictions and their affections became lasting.

August and September 1741

The months of August and September were the most remarkable of any of this year (1741), for appearances of the conviction and conversion of sinners, and great revivings, quickenings and comfort of professors. … There was an appearance of a glorious progress of the work of God upon the hearts of sinners in conviction and conversion, and great numbers, I think we have reason to hope, were brought savingly home to Christ. But this was remarkable: the work of God seemed to be almost wholly upon a new generation, those that were not come to years of discretion in that wonderful season nine years ago. …

Many who had been formerly wrought upon, and in the time of our declension had fallen into decays, and had in great measure left God, and had gone after the world, now passed under a very remarkable new work of the Spirit of God, as if they had been the subjects of a second conversion. They were first led into the wilderness and had a work of conviction, having much deeper convictions of the sins of both nature and practice than ever before. Under these convictions they were urged to strive for salvation, and the kingdom of heaven suffered violence from some of them in a far more remarkable manner than before; and after great convictions and humblings and agonising with God, they had Christ discovered to them anew, as an all sufficient Saviour and in all the glories of His grace, and in a far clearer manner than before; and with greater humility, self-emptiness, and brokenness of heart, and a purer, higher joy, and greater desires after holiness of life; but with greater self-diffidence and distrust of their treacherous hearts.

After September 1741

After September 1741, there seemed to be some abatement of these extraordinary appearances, yet they did not wholly cease, but there was something of them from time to time all the winter. About the beginning of February 1742 Mr. Buell came to this town. I was absent from home and continued so until about a fortnight after. Mr. Buell preached almost every day in the meeting-house. I had left him the free use of my pulpit. There were very marked effects of Mr. Buell's labours. The people were exceedingly moved. … When I came home I found the town in very extraordinary circumstances."

Sarah Edwards blessed

One of those who had been blessed in her soul was Jonathan Edwards' own wife. She wrote, "I felt very uneasy and unhappy at my being so low in grace. I thought I very much needed help from God. When I had been for a time earnestly wrestling for it, I felt within myself great quietness of spirit, and unusual submission to God." Later she was greatly established under the words "Who shall lay anything to the charge of God's elect?" She says, "I fell into a great flow of tears. … My safety and happiness and eternal enjoyment of God's immutable love seemed as durable and unchangeable as God Himself."

She goes on to describe similar favours under Mr. Buell's ministry. She speaks of the night of January 28th as the most blessed in her life. "All night I continued in a constant clear and lively sense of the heavenly sweetness of Christ's excellent and transcendent love, of His nearness to me and of my dearness to Him, with sweet calmness of soul in an entire rest in Him." Regarding his wife's blessing Jonathan Edwards wrote, "Now if such things are enthusiasm and the offspring of a distempered brain, let my brain be evermore possessed of that happy distemper. If this be distraction, I pray God the world of mankind may all be seized with this glorious distraction. What notions have they of true religion who reject what has been described here?"

The revival declines

Gradually in the summer of 1742 the revival declined. There were many causes of this. One was the element of enthusiasm and disorder which began to attend the meetings and was taken by many as a hallmark of the genuineness of the work. Jonathan Edwards had written a book in 1736 after the first revival entitled *A Narrative of Surprising Conversions*. As the work of Satan began to appear he produced three more works, *Distinguishing Marks of a Work of the Spirit of God* (1741), *Thoughts on the Revival of Religion in New England in 1740* and *A Treatise on Religious Affections* (1746).

Speaking of the disorders he said, "The effects and consequences of these things among us plainly show the following things; that the degree of grace is by no means to be judged of by the degree of joy or the degree of zeal, and that we cannot at all determine by these things who are gracious and who are not, and that it is not the degree of religious affections but the nature of them that are chiefly to be looked at."

It is clear that Jonathan Edwards' congregation and ministry had been the subject of the Lord's blessing, yet at the same time there had been a great failure among the people to distinguish what was the work of the enemy and what was the Lord's work. Jonathan Edwards says of this failure, "I think I have had opportunity enough to see plainly that by this the Devil has prevailed against the late Revival of religion in New England, so promising in its beginning."

Dissension among ministers and people in the New England colonies followed in the wake of the revival and Jonathan Edwards came in for very bitter attacks from some contemporary ministers who regarded his discernment as coming from a narrow, critical spirit.

CHAPTER 4

The Path of Sorrows

The Path of Sorrows

The sorrows following the 1741 revival were not the only ones which Jonathan Edwards suffered. By 1750 he was to be ejected from his pastorate at Northampton and also to have death visit his household in 1747 and 1748. He had come to know the young minister and missionary to the Indians, David Brainerd. Edwards had invited Brainerd to his home when the latter's health failed in 1747 and there at Northampton, nursed by Jonathan Edwards' daughter, Jerusha, he died on October 9th 1747. He made a blessed end, and afterwards Jonathan Edwards published the *Diary* which Brainerd had left in his hands. In the following February, Jerusha, only 18, passed away after a short illness of five days.

Of this sorrow Jonathan Edwards wrote, "It has pleased a holy and sovereign God, to take away this my dear child by death, on 14th February. … She was a person of much the same spirit with Brainerd. She had constantly taken care of and attended him in his sickness, for nineteen weeks before his death; devoting herself to it with great delight, because she looked upon him as an eminent servant of Jesus Christ.

In this time, he had much conversation with her on the things of religion; and in his dying state, often expressed to us his great satisfaction concerning the grace of God in her, and his confidence that he should meet her in heaven. . . and his high opinion of her not only as a real Christian, but as a very eminent saint; one whose soul was uncommonly fed and entertained with things which pertain to the most spiritual, experimental and distinguishing parts of religion; and one who by the temper of her mind was fitted to deny herself for God, and to do good, beyond any young woman that he knew.

She had manifested a heart uncommonly devoted to God in the course of her life, many years before her death, and said on her death bed that she had not known one minute, for several years wherein she desired to live one minute longer, for the sake of any other good in life, but doing good, living to God, and doing what might be for His glory."

Edwards Leaves Northampton

The sadness which now followed, in Edwards' having to leave Northampton after 24 years as pastor, added to which was the great blessing which had attended his ministry, is one of the great mysteries of the church of God. Why the Lord permitted the enemy to work in such a way, that a majority of his church should resist him over a matter which was so much in accord with Scripture, is hard to understand. He very graciously accepted the sorrow and went away quietly to Stockbridge, a small village, where he worked for most of the remaining years of his life among the Indians and a few English-speaking people.

Open and Strict Communion

The cause of the trouble concerned the Lord's table. His grandfather, whom he succeeded as pastor, had during his pastorate opened the Lord's table. The early Pilgrim Fathers had all been clear that only those in whose hearts there was an evident work of grace should be allowed to come to the table. Mr. Stoddard, about the year 1704, had come to regard the ordinance as a means of regeneration. This strange and totally unscriptural view of the table allowed all his parishioners except those of a known evil life to sit down to the ordinance. Jonathan Edwards accepted the call to the pastorate with this practice in the church.

Out of respect for his grandfather but not without some hesitation he allowed the practice to continue. Here was the root of his trouble, but when he became fully convinced that he could allow it to continue no longer, then he had an immense problem to handle. How was he to remove from the Lord's table large numbers of very wealthy and influential members of his church, who were mere professors of religion? In times of great blessing under the ministry, those in whose hearts the Lord had worked became very conscious of the graceless members of the church. The church became divided. Jonathan Edwards tried to bring the whole congregation to see his point of view, and in doing so lit the bitter fires of controversy around his head.

Reasons for his Departure

Writing later to a friend in Scotland he gives a full account of how he saw the events. "It is not to be wondered at that you are shocked and surprised at what has happened between me and the people of Northampton. … But, I doubt not, that God intends his own glory and the safety and prosperity of Zion.

God saw fit to bless my ministry above my predecessors and he also has seen cause to humble me more than my predecessors." He goes on to say, "The people have excelled in gifts and grace and had God extraordinarily among them; which has sensibly engendered and nourished spiritual pride, that great inlet of the devil in the hearts of men and avenue of all manner of mischief among a professing people. Spiritual pride is a monstrous thing. If it be not discerned and vigorously opposed in the beginning, it very often soon raises persons above their teachers and supposed spiritual fathers, and sets them out of the reach of all rule and instruction."

The Dangers of Publishing

He went on to speak of the dangers of publishing, as he had done, the spiritual experience of his people in *A Narrative of Surprising Conversions* (1736). "There is this danger", he said, "attending the publishing of narratives of a work of God among a people, such is the corruption that is in the hearts of men, and even of good men, that there is a great danger of making it an occasion of spiritual pride. There is great reason to think that the people of Northampton have provoked God greatly against them by trusting in their privileges and attainments. And the result may well be a warning to all God's people.

Another thing … is that the people had got so established in wrong notions… It was their method to lay almost all stress of their hopes … on the first work of the Spirit of God in their hearts … and to look but little at the abiding sense … and course of their exercises and trials of grace for evidence of their good estate. Nor had they learned ... to distinguish between impressions of the imagination and lively spiritual experience. When I came among them, I found it to be too much a practice, without discretion of distinction or occasion … to declare … their own experience, and often in a light manner."

His Own Responsibility

He goes on, "And here I desire it may be observed, that I would be so far from laying the blame of all the sorrowful things, that have come to pass, to the people, as to suppose that I have no cause of self-reflection and humiliation before God on this occasion. I am sensible that it becomes me to look on what has lately happened as an awful frown of heaven on me, as well as on the people of God. God knows the sinfulness of my heart, and the great and sinful deficiencies and offences which I have been guilty of in the course of my ministry at Northampton. ...

One thing that has contributed to bring things to such a pass was my youth, and want of more judgment and experience in the time of that extraordinary awakening about sixteen years ago. Instead of a youth, there was want of a giant, in judgment and discretion among a people in such an extraordinary state of things. In some respects my confidence in myself was a great injury to me; in other respects my diffidence of myself injured me. It was such that I durst not act my own judgment and had no strength to oppose received notions and established customs, and to testify boldly against some glaring false appearances and counterfeits of religion, till it was too late.

And by this means, as well as others, many things got footing which have proved a dreadful source of spiritual pride. … If I had had more experience and ripeness of judgment and courage, I should have guided my people in a better manner. … However, doubtless at that time there was a very glorious work of God wrought in Northampton and there were numerous instances of saving conversion, though undoubtedly many were deceived and deceived others."

His removal to Stockbridge

Edwards delivered his farewell sermon to his people on the July 1st 1750. He lived in difficult circumstances financially for nearly a year, his children having to work and many of his friends helping him, until he moved to Stockbridge, an isolated frontier village on the western borders of New England. It had had an Indian Mission since 1735 and also two schools for Indian children. Here he preached to the white congregation twice a week and to the Indians through an interpreter. He was also responsible for running the two schools. He was not free from troubles even here. White traders were making money at the expense of the Indians and thus causing bitterness, while in 1754 a war broke out in Canada between England and France which caused many of the Indians to leave the Stockbridge area.

Publishing at Stockbridge

He also continued to write and publish while here, having now more time to do so as he was free from the burden of a large pastorate. Two works which he wrote in these years were a defence of the truth and an attack on error, error he had seen growing in the New England colonies during his ministry at Northampton. The books were *A Careful and Strict Inquiry into the Prevailing Notions of the Freedom of the Will* (1754), and *The Great Christian Doctrine of Original Sin Defended* (1758). He saw those calling themselves Calvinists softening down the truth and opening the doors to freewill; therefore he resisted it.

President of Princeton and Death 1758

In 1757 he was called to be President of the Presbyterian College at Princeton, which office he took up in January 1758. Smallpox was in the town and after a vaccination Edwards died suddenly on March 22nd aged 54. His last words were, "Trust in God and ye need not fear." He had been a minister who had combined remarkable learning with remarkable grace. He was one of the great men of New England and the United States in the Puritan tradition, a direct descendant in more ways than one of the original New England settlers of the 17th century. His ministry had been greatly blessed at Northampton with revival power and there seems no doubt had had an influence on the Great Awakening that took place in England at the same period. Equally it is true of him that 'he being dead yet speaketh', as his writings have been constantly reprinted in the centuries following his death. As well as being greatly blessed as a preacher he was a theologian in the same class as John Owen. This was recognised by his fellow countrymen when he was appointed President of Princeton.

Yet as the Lord never left him to complete his ministry at Northampton but led him to the outpost at Stockbridge to preach to the Indians and to have time to write and publish for the blessing and profit of future generations, so he only held his position at Princeton for a few weeks before the Lord called him to glory. He had been led deeply in his early days into a clear view and great affection for the glories of divine sovereignty and equally in leaving Northampton and in dying at Princeton he had experimentally walked out that sovereignty and learnt that ,

> God moves in a mysterious way,
> His wonders to perform,
> He plants His footsteps in the sea,
> And rides upon the storm
>
> Deep in unfathomable mines,
> Of never failing skill,
> He treasures up His bright designs,
> And works His sovereign will.

He accomplished the work the Lord intended for him in his lifetime and since then his writings have been of immeasurable blessing to future generations yet unborn, while the Lord called him away in what, to many, seemed, the prime of life.

His Complete Works are presently available in a Two Volume Edition as well as several of his works in separate volumes from The Banner of Truth Trust U.K.

CHAPTER 5

DAVID BRAINERD
(1718 - 1747)

Youth and Conversion

Introduction

The 18th Century witnessed in America the War of Independence by which the American colonies broke away from the home country and became a separate nation. It also witnessed much contact with the Home Country in the Great Awakening in Great Britain under the ministry of George Whitefield and other godly men, who crossed the Atlantic on many occasions and preached in the New England colonies. In fact Whitefield died in America and is buried there. As Britain was the scene of the Great Awakening in the 18th century, so was the gospel greatly blessed in America in the same period.

Not only was there a great outpouring of the Spirit among English settlers in New England under the ministry of Jonathan Edwards, but the Lord also raised up His servants to take the gospel to the Indians, the indigenous population. David Brainerd, who is known mainly through the publication of his *Diary* in 1749 by his friend, Jonathan Edwards, was raised up for just such a purpose. He died at the early age of 30. He went into the ministry in 1742 and spent his preaching life among the Indians for a period of five years. His *Diary,* which was never intended for publication, reveals a deep spiritual exercise and a close walk with God. His labours followed in the track of John Eliot, "The Apostle to the Indians", minister at Roxbury near Boston for sixty years until his death in 1690 at the age of eighty-six. Eliot learnt the Indian language, reduced it to a grammatical form, preached to the Indians in their own language, translated the Bible into their own tongue, saw many converted and several churches formed. [Cf. *In Search of Freedom* J.R.Broome, pp. 139-140.]

Brainerd's ancestors were first generation settlers on his mother's side. Her father, Jeremiah Hobart, was a son of the minister, Peter Hobart, of Hingham, while her mother was a daughter of the minister, Samuel Whiting. David was the subject of much sadness in his early life. His father died in about 1727, when he was nine, and his mother in 1732, when he was about fourteen. He was the third son of his parents, who had five sons and four daughters. He was born at Haddam, a town of Hartford (County), in Connecticut. His father, Hezekiah Brainerd, was a member of the King's Council for that colony, and his grandfather on his father's side, Daniel Brainerd, had been a Justice of the Peace, and a deacon of the church at Haddam. His mother's father, Jeremiah Hobart, had been minister of the church at Haddam and died at the age of 85. When therefore David Brainerd was born on the April 20th 1718, he was born into a family having its roots deep in the New England Colonies, his grandfathers being minister and deacon in the church at Haddam in Connecticut.

Note

[The following account of David Brainerd is taken from an article which first appeared in the *Evangelical Magazine* for 1796. It is based on his own account of himself together with his *Diary* and *Journal.* Brainerd had died in the Edwards' home at Northampton in 1747, nursed at his end by their daughter, Jerusha. The year after Jonathan Edwards published David Brainerd's *Life and Diary* (1749), he himself was forced to leave his pastorate at Northampton and go to a lonely outpost on the western edge of New England at Stockbridge, where his ministry included work among the Indians. There can be little doubt that in respect of missionary work among the Indians, David Brainerd, the younger man, had a considerable influence on Jonathan Edwards.]

Childhood and Adolescence

From his childhood Brainerd experienced strong religious impressions. Being naturally of a melancholy disposition he was so terrified at the thoughts of death, that he left his childish play, and was urged by his fears to the performance of religious duties. This concern soon abated, and though he sometimes attended secret prayer, yet he lived at ease till he was 13, when a prevailing mortal sickness in the town where he resided roused him from his security. He became so fervent in his devotions that he sometimes hoped he was savingly converted. But another relapse soon showed him the deceitfulness of his heart, and the need to trust to something better than these good frames, which, at different times, had yielded him so much pleasure.

When he was about 19, he moved from Haddam, his native place, to Durham, where he worked on a farm for 12 months, frequently longing for a liberal education, with a desire to devote himself to the ministry. With this view he placed himself under the care of Mr. Fiske, pastor of the church of Haddam, applied himself to study, and became very strict and watchful over his thoughts, words, and actions. At the advice of Mr. Fiske, he totally abandoned the company of young people and associated himself with the grave and elderly. His manner of life was now exceedingly regular. He read his Bible more than twice through in less than a year, daily spent much time in prayer and other secret duties, was very attentive to the word preached, endeavouring, as much as possible, to retain it in his memory. He spent his Sunday evenings privately, with some other young people, in religious exercises; and after their meeting ended, he used to retire, and repeat to himself as much as he could recollect of the discourses of the day, which sometimes deprived him of his rest till the night was far advanced. His outward conduct being blameless, he rested entirely on his duties, though he was not sensible of it; and sometimes, feeling his affections moved in the exercises of religion, he had thoughts of joining the church.

The death of Mr. Fiske soon deprived him of the advantages he might have derived from the wisdom and grace of such a good man. He continued his studies with his brother, and still went on in the conscientious discharge of religious duties, often wondering at the levity of professors, and grieved to see them so careless and inconsistent. "Thus", he says, "I proceeded, a considerable length, on a self-righteous foundation, and should have been utterly lost and undone, had not the mercy of God prevented".

Conviction

In the beginning of the winter, 1738, as he was walking, on a Sabbath morning, in a retired situation, for the purposes of meditation and prayer, it pleased God, all of a sudden, so to impress his mind with a sense of his danger, and the wrath he had deserved, that he was struck with astonishment, and the pleasure arising from all his former good frames instantly vanished. He became so cast down from a view of his sin and vileness that he kept much alone, envying the birds and beasts their happiness, because they were not exposed to eternal misery, as he saw himself to be. Mountains of difficulties obstructed his hopes of mercy. The work of conversion appeared so great, that though he almost despaired of being the happy subject of it, yet he prayed to God, and performed his religious duties with more earnestness than ever, hoping, by some means or other, to make the case better. Hundreds of times he renounced all pretences of any worth in his duties, confessing that he deserved nothing for the very best of them but eternal condemnation; yet still he cherished a latent hope of recommending himself to God by the performance of them; for when he prayed earnestly, and his heart seemed, in some measure, to melt, he hoped God would hear such sincere cries, and be moved to pity him. And when he mourned for sin, he thought he could, in some measure, venture on the mercy of God in Christ; concluding, when he felt any enlargement in duty, that he had advanced a considerable step towards heaven.

Whatever qualifications he supposed others possessed, before their union with Christ, these he strove to obtain, in order to recommend himself to the divine favour. Whilst he imagined there was some appearance of goodness in his prayer and repentance, he was greatly encouraged, and thought he should soon be reconciled to God; but when he perceived the vileness of his nature, and his inability to deliver himself from the justice of a sovereign God, his distress revived, the discovery being too painful for him to endure.

When the fervour of his devotion became languid

for any considerable time together, convictions of sin generally seized him with greater violence. One night particularly, when he was walking alone, he had such a view of his sins, that he feared the ground would suddenly cleave asunder under his feet, and his soul quickly go down into hell. Though such distress was not uncommon when he had a lively sense of his own depravity, yet he greatly dreaded the loss of convictions, lest he should return to a state of carnal security and insensibility of impending wrath; this fear made him very cautious not to stifle the motions of the Spirit of God. But so deceitful is the human heart, that when at any time he thought the degree of his convictions was considerable, it produced such confident hope that he should soon make some notable advances towards deliverance as eased his mind and soon generated that coldness and insensibility he so much dreaded.

Frequently he imagined himself humbled, and prepared for saving mercy, and no less frequently did his fancied hopes disappear. At length, repeatedly disappointed in his expectation, his corrupt heart was irritated; the frame of his mind became horrible; he entered into a contest with the Almighty, disapproving of His dealings with mankind, and quarrelling with His holy law, that looked upon the thoughts and intents of the heart, as unreasonably rigid and severe. He found great fault with the imputation of Adam's sin to his posterity and often wished there had been some other way of salvation than by Jesus Christ, or that God would have permitted men to obtain the blessings of it by sincere prayers and endeavours, which he thought they could perform, and not by faith alone, which he knew was beyond the power of man to exercise, it being the gift of God, and which He alone could give.

To the sovereignty of God he felt much opposition. Some passages in the 9th chapter of the Romans were a constant trouble to him. If they occurred to his mind, when he was in a comfortable frame, his pleasure vanished and even when he thought he was almost humbled, and resigned to God's will, if he happened to read, or think on them, his enmity against divine sovereignty was immediately aroused.

The blasphemy that arose upon these occasions made him the more afraid of God, and drove him farther from all hope of reconciliation. At the same time, the Spirit of God was so powerfully at work with his soul that the conviction of his lost estate was sometimes so clear and manifest, as if it had been declared to him in so many words. It is done, it is done, it is forever impossible to deliver yourself! The greatest distress immediately followed. At the sight of his lost condition his soul recoiled; yet he dared not venture himself, as a helpless sinner, into the hands of God, to be at the disposal of His sovereign pleasure. He trembled to contemplate this important truth, that he was 'dead in trespasses and sins'. But when he had put away these views of himself, he was unhappy, and desired to have the same discoveries renewed, fearing greatly lest God should give him over to be lost at last.

Christ Formed in his Heart

After a considerable time spent in such painful exercises of mind, while he was walking one morning as usual, in a solitary place, he at once perceived that all his endeavours to procure deliverance were utterly in vain, and was now fully convinced that he was totally lost. Instead of blaming himself that he had not done more while he had the opportunity, he saw that, let him have done what he would, all would have been ineffectual. The former tumult of his mind was now quieted, and he was eased of the distress he felt while struggling in opposition to divine sovereignty.

He had the greatest certainty that his state was forever miserable, for all that he could do, and wondered that he had never realised it before. His ideas respecting his religious duties were quite altered. Instead of thinking that the more he did, the greater claim he had to God's favour, or, at least, that it would be more hard if God should finally reject him, he now saw that there was no necessary connection between his prayers and divine mercy, that God was under no obligation to bestow grace upon him, because he asked it, self-interest being the motive which induced him to pray, and not any respect to His glory.

A few days later he went, thoughtful and sorrowful, to the same solitary place, and attempted to pray, but found no heart to engage in it or any other duty; he was disconsolate from a fear that the Spirit of God had quite forsaken him, yet not the subject, as before, of painful distress. Having in vain endeavoured to pray, for near half an hour, as he was walking in a dark, thick wood, his soul was favoured with a view of unspeakable glory, not accompanied with any external brightness or splendour, but an inward view of the nature and perfections of God, such as he had never before experienced.

His mind was not directed to the contemplation of any one particular person in the Trinity; the glory of the Godhead he then beheld, and his soul was filled with joy unspeakable; he was inwardly pleased that He should be God over all for ever and ever. So delighted was he with His excellency, loveliness, greatness and other perfections, that his thoughts were quite absorbed, at least, to such a degree, that he lost all concern about his own salvation, and scarcely reflected there was such a creature as himself in existence.

Such was the wonderful and unexpected manner in which he was brought to exalt God, and set Him on the throne; aiming principally and ultimately at His honour and glory as King of kings. His mind was at peace. He felt himself in a new world, everything appearing with a different aspect. In the way of salvation he discovered such infinite wisdom, suitableness, and excellency, that he was surprised how he could ever have thought of any other, or adhered to his own performances in preference to it.

After such sovereign favour, could he have been saved by any of his own works or duties, or any other way he had previously conceived, he would have rejected the very thought of them. His wonder was that the whole world did not embrace so great salvation through the righteousness of Christ. The sweet relish of what he had then enjoyed continued with him many days. But the most eminent saints must not expect the love of their espousals to last always whilst in this present world, perhaps more so where such as David Brainerd are troubled with a melancholy spirit. It was not long therefore before his mind was again much in darkness, though the darkness was graciously removed before long.

CHAPTER 6

Steps in Providence

Yale College 1739

At the beginning of September, 1739 he entered himself at Yale College, in New Haven; but not without reluctance, fearful lest, amidst the many temptations to which he might be exposed, he should not be able to lead a life of strict religion. During the vacation, before he went to live in the college, he was spending some time in prayer and self-examination; when it pleased the Lord to visit him with such bright manifestations of Himself and His grace, that his soul was unspeakably refreshed with heavenly enjoyments. Many passages of Scripture were opened to his mind with such divine clearness and power, as produced full conviction of its being the word of God. Through the whole of the following Winter he enjoyed considerable blessing in his soul. Having caught the measles, an illness which spread in the college, he returned in January to Haddam. A few days before he was taken ill, he mourned much the absence of the Comforter; and though he cried earnestly to God for help, he found no immediate relief. But while he was walking alone, in a very quiet spot, engaged in meditation and prayer, he was favoured with such a season of refreshment from the presence of the Lord, as lifted him far above the fear of death, and filled his soul with a greater delight than all the enjoyments that earth can afford. And though in his illness his life was despaired of, yet for him death was disarmed of its sting.

When he recovered, he continued his studies with such close attention as proved damaging to his health. Feeling his weakness, and seeing that he began to bring up blood, he took the advice of his tutor, and gave up his studies from August to November; spending much of the time in prayer and self-examination, sometimes mourning bitterly over his exceeding sinfulness and vileness, and, at other times, rejoicing in a lively sense of the Lord's favour, feeling his heart unusually drawn out in grateful returns of affection and praise. At the same time he felt an exceeding great tenderness and fervent affection for all mankind; his soul and all the powers of it seemed, as it were, to dissolve in softness and compassion. Such love and joy cast out fear and he longed for the perfection of grace and glory.

Persuaded that college life had proved spiritually harmful to him, his recovery afforded him little comfort. On the contrary, could his desire have been granted, he would rather have died, in the frame of mind he then possessed, than return to a place where he feared his communion with God would be interrupted. This holy jealousy proved beneficial. It made him watchful, lest he should fall into his old temptation, and suffer his heart to be drawn sway from the ardent pursuit of heavenly objects, by his ambition to excel in learning.

For the space of six weeks after his return he experienced, almost daily, the power of religion and walked in the light of God's reconciled countenance. About the end of January, however, he grew more cold and dull, through attention to study; but when a general awakening began to spread itself over the college during the following month, his soul was abundantly quickened.

Expelled from Yale 1742

While thus, with his progress in spiritual things, he was making considerable advances in literature, a circumstance occurred, painful in its nature, but very important in its consequences. One day, as he was in the Hall with two or three of the students, whom he often met for a talk, one of them asked his opinion of a Mr. Whittelsey, one of the tutors, who had been uncommonly pathetic in prayer. Brainerd, leaning upon his chair, replied, "He has no more grace than this chair." A junior student, who was near the door, over-hearing the words, and suspecting that they were spoken of one of the tutors, mentioned it to a woman belonging to the town; who immediately went and informed the Rector of the college.

Mr. Brainerd's friends were sent for and interrogated, and compelled by threats to declare the name of the person to whom the words were applied.

The governors insisted on his humbling himself before the whole college, making confession in the same public manner as was required of those who had been guilty of some notorious crime. With this demand he refused to comply, but readily acknowledged the impropriety of the expression, and asked pardon of Mr. Whittelsey for the liberty he had taken with his character, though it was only in a private conversation with his most intimate friends. For this offence, discovered by means so unjustifiable, he was expelled from the college at the beginning of 1742. Another charge was that he had once attended the preaching of Mr. Tennant, a minister of Christ greatly blessed in the revival, though the rector had refused to give him leave.

Such violent proceeding against so good a man gave great offence to many. His own mind was much affected by it, fearing that the academic censure would prove injurious to his future ministry; but he conducted himself on the trying occasion in the most Christian manner, and was ever after more ready to blame himself than to condemn others; though so long as he lived, he considered himself, as to the management of the affair, much abused. But for this painful event, he would have taken his degree on the next commencement day with his classmates, and appeared at the head of them, and would, probably, have proceeded to the highest academic honours. Mortifying as the disappointment was, it rather increased than diminished his desire for the ministry. He therefore immediately placed himself under the Rev. Mills of Ripton, that he might pursue his studies and qualify himself for the work.

Work among the Indians

About this time he first appears to have cherished a hope that he should one day be employed, as an instrument in the conversion of the heathen. Previously to his expulsion, he makes no mention in his writings of such a design, but ever afterwards his views seem to be principally directed to that object. He now began to wrestle earnestly with God for the salvation of the heathen, and for the extension of the kingdom of Christ in the world. He became more fervent than ever in his private devotions, and set apart whole days for fasting and prayer, beseeching the Lord to prepare him for the work of the ministry, and in due time to send him into his harvest, earnestly interceding for the salvation of immortal souls, and particularly pleading for the illumination and conversion of the poor heathen.

On these occasions he was frequently enabled to strive with God in prayer to such a degree that his body was covered with perspiration, even when the air was cool, and his worship performed in the shade. So abundant was his compassion towards the souls of others, that he felt greater pleasure when interceding for them than in any other part of prayer. But amidst these spiritual exercises, he complains of the operations of spiritual pride and had such discoveries of his own vileness that he humbled himself in the dust before God, wondering that He would suffer any of his creatures to feed and sustain him; or that He should dispose the hearts of any of His people to notice him, and shew him kindness. Viewing the boundless mercy of God, in pardoning all his iniquities, and clearing him from his exceeding filthiness, and overwhelmed with a sense of His infinite condescension in favouring such a worm with His presence; he was willing if God should so order it, to be banished from his native land among the heathen, and endure sufferings of any kind, or even death itself, provided he might be instrumental in doing good to their souls.

Preach the Word

The time was now fast approaching when God, who had endowed him with special grace, was about to employ him in special services. Among other advantages which he derived from his present situation, he had frequent opportunities of visiting several ministers. They, seeing his grace and maturity, gave him all possible encouragement, and on the July 29th 1742 he was examined by the Association assembled at Danbury who were so satisfied with his learning, knowledge and religious experience, that he received from them a licence to preach the gospel.

Blessed with peculiar talents, favoured with the most intimate communication with God, and humbled under a sense of his own depravity, Brainerd entered upon the arduous work of the ministry, preaching occasionally in the pulpits of his friends, from the day he was licensed, till the providence of God opened for him a door of utterance among the heathen.

The day after he was licensed, he rode to Southbury and preached, where he enjoyed much of the comfortable presence of God, both in his prayer and sermon; and for several days he continued in a sweet tranquillity of mind, being sometimes refreshed with the hope of seeing the heathen coming to Christ. But on the 12th August, while he was at a place near Kent, in the western borders of Connecticut, where there was a number of Indians, his soul was exercised with the most severe conflict. He had no power to pray; his hopes, that God would send him afar off among the heathen, vanished; his spirit was so exceedingly depressed with a sense of his vileness, that he seemed in his own eyes worse than any devil. He could not conceive why God permitted him to live.

The trial had lasted all that morning and the preceding night. About ten o'clock the people assembled, and he was forced to ascend the pulpit. Contrary to his expectations, the Lord so favoured him with His presence, and assisted him in praying and preaching, that he spoke with power; some of the Indians present cried out in deep distress, and all appeared greatly affected. This revived his hopes, and induced him to hire a woman to keep a school for their instruction.

However strongly his mind was impressed with a sense of his insufficiency and unworthiness, all who heard him were persuaded God had raised him up for great usefulness. His remarkable concern for the conversion of the heathen could not be concealed; and on the November 19th 1742, he received an invitation from the Rev. Pemberton of New York to come there as soon as possible, and meet the correspondents of The Society in Scotland, for the Propagation of Christian Knowledge, and consult with them about the affairs of the neighbouring Indians.

This was a solemn message. He felt more than ever the weight of the important subject for which the interview was desired, but was enabled to cast his burden upon the Lord, earnestly requesting His help and direction. The correspondents were satisfied with his Christian experience and knowledge of the truth, and engaged him for the work. Their design was to send him to the Indians at the Forks of Delaware. But as the winter season was then approaching, which in that part of America is remarkably cold, it was thought best for him to delay his journey till the following spring.

The interval, however, was not spent unprofitably for himself or others. He conversed occasionally with his friends; he read much, prayed much, and preached often. Considering himself as for ever devoted to the work in which he had engaged, and expecting soon to go and spend the remainder of his life among savages in the wilderness, he began to think how he might glorify God most with the property left him by his father. No better way occurred to his thoughts than to educate some young man for the ministry. He accordingly made an offer to a person whom he thought most promising, and having given him some previous education, sent him to college at his sole expense.

CHAPTER 7

Among the Indians

Kaunaumeek April 1743

The ministers whom Brainerd had met at Woodbridge in march had received information that there was a conflict between the white people and the Indians at Delaware, concerning ownership of land. They supposed that this would be a hindrance to the preaching of the gospel, so, as he was preparing for his journey to Delaware, they gave him new directions, and sent him among the Indians at Kaunaumeek.

Kaunaumeek was a place in the province of New York, in the woods between Stockbridge and Albany, and about twenty miles distant from each of these towns. Here he arrived on April 1st 1743 and was kindly received by the Indians, who soon became seriously attentive to his instruction. He stayed with them the best part of a year, but was subject to great gloominess and distress of mind, being exposed to many hardships and difficulties, sleeping on straw, in a wretched hovel, and living on food of a most ordinary kind, even reduced at times to hunger as no food could be had from a distance of less than sixteen to eighteen miles.

He ascribes the favourable reception he met with, to the long-continued labours of the Rev. Sergeant among some of the same tribe, by whose report their prejudices were, in a great measure, removed, and their minds prepared to entertain the truths of Christianity. He immediately endeavoured to teach them the nature of the fall and recovery in the most plain and easy manner, addressing them by an interpreter, a young educated Indian, who had been taught the truth by Rev. Sergeant, and was able to read and write well.

After he had been there some months he composed and, by the help of his interpreter, translated into their own language, several Psalms and forms of prayer, adapted to their circumstances and capacities, and which he learned to pronounce so well, that he could sing and pray with them in their own tongue.

When they had gained some acquaintance with such truths as he thought were necessary to be previously known, he gave them an historical account of God's dealings with the Jews, and explained some of their rites, ceremonies, and sacrifices, leading them gradually on to the birth, life, miracles, sufferings, death, resurrection, and ascension of Christ, and the consequent outpouring of the Holy Spirit. And having prepared the way by this general view of things, he regularly expounded in the evenings the Gospel of Matthew.

Besides these instructions, he had, by the consent of the Commissioners, instituted a school for children and young people, and appointed his interpreter to teach them English attending himself, as often as he could, to give them serious exhortations; and in a short time he had the pleasure of seeing that they made considerable headway. A few seemed awakened to a concern for deliverance from their miserable state by nature, and an outward reformation appeared in the lives and manners of most. Their Idolatrous sacrifices were laid aside, their heathenish customs considerably abated, and their drunkenness somewhat lessened. Many showed a regard for the Sabbath, yet, after all these hopeful appearances, there were things so discouraging that he could not say he had any real evidences of their being renewed in the spirit of their minds, and savingly converted to God.

The River Delaware April 1744

Having had an interview with the ministers in the winter, and informing them of these things, with a view to some new arrangement, he was ordered by them in April 1744 to go to another tribe of Indians near the river Delaware. This being at a considerable distance from Kaunaumeek, he began to dispose of his books, and make preparation for the journey. For though he must have felt much regret at having laboured so long to so little or no purpose, and though he had been asked to settled at Millington, near his native town, as well as having received a pressing invitation from the people at East Hampton, a most pleasant town in Long Island; and though he knew that in the place where he was going he would be subject to extreme hardships yet so firmly was he bent on the work upon which he had set out, that he determined to go forward.

But his Indians, on hearing his intentions to leave, were sad, and did all they could to persuade him to stay with them. He sympathised, and advised them, as they were so few, to remove to Stockbridge, where they might be instructed under the ministry of Rev. Sergeant. This they readily agreed to do; and on Sunday, April 29th he took his leave of them in a farewell sermon in Rev. Sergeant's pulpit at Stockbridge, where most of them had then arrived having been well accommodated with land.

Leaving Stockbridge on the following Thursday, he set out on his journey, calling on his friends in the various places through which he passed. Finding a number of Indians at a place called Minnisinks, he offered to instruct them in the truths of Christianity. The king of the tribe from whom he asked leave to do this, laughed and, turning on his heel, went away. Brainerd followed him to his house and repeated his request, but he declined to answer and referred the matter to another Indian, who appeared a reasonable man. "Why", he said, "should you desire the Indians to become Christians, seeing the Christians are so much worse than the Indians? The Christians lie, steal, and drink worse than the Indians. They first taught the Indians to drink. They steal to such a degree, that their rulers are obliged to hang them for it, and even that is not sufficient to deter others. But none of the Indians were ever hanged for stealing. We will not consent, therefore, to become Christians, lest we should be as bad as they. We will live as our fathers lived, and go where our fathers are when we die."

In vain Brainerd endeavoured to convince him that some who are called Christians are not Christians in heart. He became angry, and when he was asked by Brainerd if he was willing for him to come and see them again, he replied, that they would be willing to see him again, as a friend, if he would not desire them to become Christians. Saddened by this reply, and grieved that the injuries which these Indians had received from evil men calling themselves by the Christian name should have engendered such prejudices, he said goodbye with an aching heart and pursued his journey, arriving on May 13th at a place in the province of Pennsylvania, called by the Indians Sakhauwotung, within the Forks of Delaware.

Sakhauwotung May 1744

Here, by consent of their king, he pitched his tent among a few Indians, well disposed and very attentive, There were not more than thirteen inhabited houses, and these lay several miles distant from each other because several of those who formerly lived there had moved farther back into the country. As a result he could collect only a few of them together, amounting to no more than twenty or twenty-five people. Towards the end of the summer, however, the number increased to about forty, which encouraged him greatly.

Hearing of a few Indians about 30 miles westward, he went and found them preparing to move towards the Susquahannah River, their permanent place of residence. He was able to preach to them twice; and though at first they feared he had some evil design against them, having before suffered injuries from the white people, they were pleased with his company and his conversation. Furthermore, they asked him to visit them at their homes in Susquahannah and give them further instruction.

This invitation gave him great encouragement, and he agreed, as late as October, to undertake the tiring journey. Having travelled three days, and slept two nights in the open, he came to their settlement on the banks of the Susquahannah River. They were about to set out on their general hunting for the season but delayed it four days, on each of which he was able to preach to them twice, besides conversing with them, and endeavouring to overcome their objections to Christianity. After this it was agreed by them all that he should renew his visit in the following spring. Hoping that God was thus preparing their hearts to receive His Word, he returned to his people at Delaware.

Here events occurred which caused him great uneasiness. The Indians, notwithstanding the pains he had taken with them, engaged in an idolatrous feast and dance; nor could they be dissuaded from it by his entreaties. This was not the only occasion he had been tempted by these things, the result of which considerably depressed him, and he began to entertain little hope of success. But having finished a hut which he had built to live in for the sake of retirement, he determined to cast himself at the feet of his Saviour, and to spend his time in fasting and prayer that he might implore mercy for these people.

But the time was fast approaching when the days of his mourning should be ended. The Lord had indeed brought him into the wilderness, but he soon found this valley of Achor was to be a door of hope. In a few days he had the pleasure of hearing his interpreter, for whose conversion he had so greatly longed, express an earnest concern for his soul. This brought new care; his hope was mingled with fear, and he besought the Lord that the work might be real and lasting. Similar impressions he found were being made on others, who shed many tears under his preaching; and particularly an old man supposed to be 100 years old who was deeply affected. Brainerd tells us, however, he had no reason to conclude they were partakers of true and saving grace, but were only the subjects of conviction.

A Missionary Journey

Desirous of fulfilling his promise to the Indians at Susquahannah, he set out with his interpreter at the beginning of May 1745, enduring great hardship and weariness; they were obliged to sleep one night in the open air, exposed to wind and rain, and to travel on foot the next day driving their horses before them, which they could neither ride nor lead, as they were so sick with a poisonous herb they had eaten the night before.

After reaching Susquahannah he proceeded about a hundred miles along the banks of the River, visiting several settlements, and preaching to them by different interpreters. Sometimes he was discouraged by the opposition he met to the Christian religion, and sometimes encouraged by the reception of others, and their willingness to be instructed. Here he met with some of the Indians who had been his hearers at Kaunaumeek, who both saw and heard him with strong expressions of joy.

Having spent some weeks in this laborious work, sleeping on the ground, and frequently in the open air, he was taken with fever, which nearly proved fatal. But it pleased God to give him sufficient strength to reach the hut of an Indian trader where, with the Lord's blessing, and without the aid of medicine, he recovered, and on May 30th, after a journey of three hundred and forty miles, returned to his own people.

'In Labours More Abundant'

For two years he had now laboured with very little, if any, success. He perceived the Indians much prejudiced against his preaching in certain places owing to the treatment they had received at the hands of those who only bore the name of Christian. They were closely attached to their own customs and traditions, particularly to their belief that they were not made by the same God who made the white people, but by another who commanded they should live by hunting, and must therefore abide with their forefathers in life and death.

In addition, the manner of their living was a great obstacle to keeping in touch with them as they were continually roving from place to place, so that the men were scarcely ever to be met, except about six weeks before and in the season of planting their corn, and two months after the harvest. Brainerd also had to contend with the hardships and weariness of frequent journeys in the wild, the poor food and lodging, the difficulty of speaking to people of a strange tongue. He felt the absence of a Christian companion, and fellow-labourer, though Jesus sent His disciples by two and two. So we need not wonder if he had even entertained the thought of withdrawing from the work in which he had almost despaired of success. But even now brighter days were ahead.

CHAPTER 8

Cast the Net on the Right

Cast the Net on the Right Side

Like the disciples, Brainerd had been toiling hard, and had caught nothing, when it pleased the Lord to direct him where to cast the net for a successful draught. Whilst visiting several ministers in New Jersey for the recovery of his health, he heard from them of a few Indians in that province, at a place called Crossweeksung. Feeling a strong impulse to go there he set out and arrived on June 19th 1745. They were a little company of four women and eight children, but they heard his word, and he indicated his willingness to preach to them the day following. In order that others might hear also they travelled from ten to fifteen miles to tell their friends, so that on his return he found an increased company who listened with remarkable attention. These having invited others, he had within the course of the week the pleasure of being surrounded by a congregation of about forty people.

But what gave him greater pleasure was the considerable concern they expressed for the safety of their souls, and the earnest as well as affectionate manner in which they requested him to preach twice a day. In spite of his low state of health he could not resist their invitation, being persuaded that God had inclined them thus to enquire the way of salvation. He had likewise the satisfaction of seeing the providence of God concur with their wishes, for they were able to kill three deer, which proved to be a source of food, without which they could not have stayed, as many of them were at a considerable distance from their homes.

Having preached among them for a fortnight, he was pleased to see the degree of knowledge to which some of them had attained. Feeling it to be now his duty, as soon as health permitted, to revisit his own people at the Forks of Delaware, about 80 miles away, he left them, but with great reluctance. On taking his leave of them they promised they would continue to meet with him, and also collect together other Indians, who lived further away, to receive the benefit of his ministry. One told him with tears, that she wished God would change her heart and another that, she wanted to find Christ. An old man, one of their chiefs, being in great distress of soul, wept bitterly.

Crossweeksung - The Power of the Spirit

He returned to the Indians at Delaware, and preached on July 14$^{th.}$ The Indians shed many tears during the service, the Spirit being evidently present, convincing many of them of their sins. Here he baptized his interpreter and his wife, who were his first fruits among the heathen. He then, after giving them particular advice and counsel, left them for a while to return to the flock in New Jersey. He was happy to find that the impressions made on his first visit to Crossweeksung had not faded, and that many of them were still under deep concern for an interest in Christ.

Without waiting until the more distant ones could be brought in, he preached to about twenty, and was enabled, he says, to set forth the Lord Jesus Christ as a compassionate Saviour who invited distressed sinners to come unto Him. Being invited by a neighbouring minister to assist in the administration of the Lord's Supper, he took some of those who were affected with him, and they were much moved by what they saw and heard. A change in their manner now began to appear. In the evening they would not eat till they had sent for him to ask a blessing on their food. When he reminded them how, in times past, they had feasted in honour of devils, and neglected to give God thanks, they wept abundantly.

The next day, in concluding preaching, he addressed himself to the Indians in particular, who sat in a part of the house by themselves, and the Lord applied the Word to them with power, so that he found them at night enquiring what they should do to be saved, except one woman, convinced under his preaching in June, who was set at liberty and filled with the love of Christ. Their whole conversation among themselves now turned on these subjects, and so tender were they in their consciences that a few words about the concerns of their souls produced many tears and sighs.

On the following day he preached from 1 John 4;10,

"Not that we loved God, but that He loved us", to about fifty-five persons, forty of whom were capable of attending divine service with understanding. Great was their attention, and the divine influence was truly wonderful. The more he set forth the compassion of God in sending His Son to suffer for the sins of men the more they felt their helplessness. Two Indians in particular obtained relief, and when asked what more they wanted God to do for them they replied that they wanted Christ to wash their hearts clean. What Brainerd himself felt is better conceived than expressed. He stood rebuked for his former unbelieving fears, and tasted joy mingled with astonishment. "Surprising", says he, "were now the doings of the Lord, that I can say no less of this day, and I need say no more of it, than that the arm of the Lord was powerfully revealed."

This was an auspicious beginning, but it was only the morning of a glorious noon. For two days after, while he was preaching with uncommon freedom to about sixty-five persons on the 'gospel feast' Luke 14; 16-23, there was much visible concern among them but afterwards when he spoke to those whom he perceived to be most distressed, the power of God seemed to rest on the assembly like a mighty wind. Almost all persons, of whatever age, were bowed down with concern. The most stubborn hearts were now obliged to bend.

A principal man among them now lamented his guilty state. Another who had been a murderer and a conjuror among them, as well as being a notorious drunkard, was brought to cry for mercy with many tears. Even out of doors numbers were to be seen praying freely as if they had been alone in seclusion. Those who had been awakened before complained chiefly of the badness of their hearts, and those newly awakened of the badness of their lives and actions. Those who had lately obtained relief were filled with comfort, and seemed to rejoice in Christ Jesus; and some of them taking their weeping friends by the hand, told them of the goodness of Christ and the happiness that is to be enjoyed in Him.

Notwithstanding his debilitated frame and great exertions during the six days he had laboured there, he remained another three weeks, labouring like the husbandman in the time of harvest, fatigued with reaping his fruits, the ample recompense of all his toil. His Indian hearers increased until they reached ninety-five. When they met a blessed influence spread through the assembly. Many of the white people, who only came to laugh and revile, were pricked to the heart, and became humble suppliants for mercy, although in most of his discourses he addressed himself to the consciences of these baptized heathens, and frequently preached entirely to them here and at Delaware to which place he now returned after taking an affectionate farewell of the flock at Crossweeksung.

The Work Continues

Opposition now appeared. Those that were born after

the flesh began to persecute those that were born after the Spirit. Some of the Indians at Delaware who had always refused to hear him preach, raged against those who attended his ministry, reviled them, and scoffed bitterly at Christianity. Leaving here on September 9th, he pursued his journey to preach at two more principal places along the river. But "the wind bloweth where it listeth", and sovereignty presides in the dispensation of mercy, as he was to be once more reminded, for no apparent good resulted.

Much distressed he returned to Delaware and invited his people there to go with him to Crossweeksung which they did, and found the same divine influence as had been formerly experienced. "O!" he exclaimed, "what a difference between those I have lately served. To be with them was as if I was banished from God and all His people: to be with these is like being admitted into His family, and to the enjoyment of His divine presence." During three services the next day the same power was felt, and the most desirable affection in the people. Scarcely a dry eye was seen among them, yet there was nothing boisterous or unseemly.

Did our limits permit it would be pleasing to recount all the blessed effects of his ministry in and around this district. [See Extracts from Brainerd's *Journal* in Chapter 9 for a more detailed account.] The influence of the Spirit of God was often remarkable; some seasons were special seasons of grace. One of these was on the 29th of December 1745, after he had been preaching on the new birth, when a number of white people were also gathered with the Indians.

It was a Sabbath day, and after the services were over many followed him to his house with tears in their eyes, asking what they must do to be saved. They flocked together, and were seized with general concern so that it appeared as if the Lord had bowed the heavens and come down. In these solemn circumstances he continued addressing them, together or alone, from the late morning until seven in the evening, with but little intermission. Nor could the attempts of the white people to frighten or prejudice them impede the work, though they propagated many evil reports respecting Brainerd and his intentions.

In the course of eleven months he baptized nearly forty adults; at the same time, he informs us "there were many of sufficient knowledge and seriousness to render them proper subjects of baptism". But he deferred the ordinance till the evidences of saving change should be more clear, fearing that a scandal would be brought on the Christian profession if any should fall away into idolatry again.

He instituted a school under the care of a godly person, who taught between thirty to forty children during the day, and frequently near twenty adults in the evening. The children were soon able to read the Psalms and the New Testament, and to repeat the Assembly's *Shorter Catechism.*

On March 24th 1746, he numbered the Indians and found they amounted to one hundred and fifty, though at his first coming they only numbered ten. As their existence depended principally on hunting which obliged them to be often absent, and exposed to many temptations, and as there was the likelihood of their numbers increasing he saw how important it was that they should become acquainted with cultivation, and able to raise the necessities and comforts of life among themselves.

He therefore advised them to remove from their present barren spot to a place about fifteen miles distant, to clear and cultivate the land, and build a little town where they might live together and regularly attend the worship of God. He lived to see this accomplished, and a church of Christ established to whom he administered the ordinances of the gospel, eating and drinking with them in commemoration of the death of their common Lord, and performing all the endearing offices of a pastor and father in Christ.

In the winter of 1746, through illness hastened by a lengthy journey he felt prompted to make to some of the Indians, he was laid up for four months at Elizabeth Town, two miles from Cranberry, where his Indians resided. Recovering a little he rode to them on 18th March 1747, and after singing and expounding a Psalm he prayed with them. This was the last meeting he ever had with his people.

His work done

Soon after, on the advice of friends, he set out on a journey to New England, hoping his health might yet be recovered by a change of air and riding. But it pleased God, who had approved and prospered his work to take him to Himself. On October 9th 1747, after he had lingered on a bed of sickness at Northampton in New England in the home of Jonathan Edwards, during which time he experienced strong consolations, he died, surrounded by affectionate friends, among whom was his brother John, who succeeded him in his pastoral office, and refreshed him in his dying moments by the recent tidings he brought to him from his dear Indians.

William Bradford, the leader of the Pilgrim Fathers says of the first Pilgrims in his *Journal*, "An inward zeal they had of laying some good foundation, or at least to make some way thereunto for the propagating and advancing of the kingdom of Christ in those remote parts of the world; yea, though they should even be as a stepping stone unto others for the performing of so great a work." Here, over a century later, after some tragic conflicts with the indigenous Indian population, resulting in many Indians and settlers being killed, at least one of the forebears of the Pilgrims had given his life in the fulfilment of one of the desires of the Pilgrim Fathers, when they left Leyden in the Netherlands and migrated to New England. The Pilgrim fathers were indeed as "a stepping stone" "for performing of so great a work" as that accomplished by David Brainerd and his predecessor John Eliot in taking the gospel among the Indians.

CHAPTER 9

Extracts from Part II of the *Journal* of David Brainerd

[Works of Jonathan Edwards 2 Vols London 1865 Tenth Edition. Reprinted Banner of Truth Vol. 2 pp.401 - 415]

David Brainerd kept both a *Diary* and a *Journal.* The first he kept for his own benefit; the second was kept by order of The Honourable Society (in Scotland) for Propagating Christian Knowledge, who had sent him and supported him in his work among the Indians. Both the *Diary* and the *Journal* appear in the two volume edition of *The Works of Jonathan Edwards* London 1865. They are also printed in *The Life and Diary of David Brainerd,* edited by Jonathan Edwards, printed in 1949 by the Moody Press Chicago, U.S.A.

Part II November 24th 1745 - June 19th 1746. At Crossweeksung and the Forks of Delaware.

December 21st 1745

My people having now attained to a considerable degree of knowledge in the principles of Christianity,

I thought it proper to set up a lecture among them. This evening attempted something in this form proposing questions to them agreeable to the Assembly's *Shorter Catechism*, receiving their answers, and then explaining as appeared necessary upon each question. After which I made some improvement of the whole. They were able to readily answer many important points much better than my expectations.

Lord's Day December 22nd

Discoursed upon the young man in the Gospel, Matthew 19;16-22. God made it a seasonable word. There were some Indians there newly come to the place who had lived among Quakers. Being more civilised, and conformed to the English manners, they had imbibed some of the Quakers' errors, especially this fundamental one; that if men will but live soberly and honestly, according to the dictates of their own consciences (or the light within), there is then no danger or doubt of their salvation.

These I found much worse to deal with than those who are wholly under pagan darkness, who have no pretences to Christianity, nor any self-righteousness to stand upon. However they all, except one, now seemed convinced that this sober life was not sufficient to salvation, since Christ Himself had declared it so to the young man.

December 25th

The Indians having been used upon Christmas day

to drink and revel among some of the white people, I thought it proper to call them together and discourse upon divine things; which I accordingly did from the Parable of the Barren Fig Tree, Luke 13; 6-9. A divine influence, I am persuaded, accompanied the Word, by shocking and rousing at heart, as it seemed, several stupid creatures, that were scarce ever moved with any concern before. The power attending the words seemed to have the power of the earthquake rather than the whirlwind. Their judgments appeared to be powerfully convinced by the conquering influence of divine truths. What liveliness and strict attention! They seemed to watch and wait for the dropping of God's word. Afterwards I discoursed upon the duty of husbands and wives, from Ephesians 5; 22-23, and have reason to think the Word was in season.

December 26th

This evening I was visited by a person under great spiritual exercise the most remarkable instance of this kind I ever saw. She was a woman of (I believe) more than fourscore years, and appeared to be much broken and very childish through age, so that it seemed impossible for man to instil into her mind any notions of divine things, much less to give her any doctrinal instruction because she seemed incapable of being taught. She was led by the hand into my house and appeared in extreme anguish. I asked her what ailed her. She answered that her heart was distressed and she feared she should never find Christ. I asked her when she began to be concerned, with several other questions relating to her distress.

To all of which she answered, for substance, to this effect: that she had heard me preach many times, but never knew anything about it, never "felt it in her heart" till the last Sabbath; and then it came (she said) "all one as if a needle had been thrust into her heart". Since which time, she had no rest day nor night. She added that on the evening before Christmas, a number of Indians being together at the house where she was and discoursing about Christ, their talk pricked her heart so that she could not sit up, but fell down on her bed.

At this time she went away (as she expressed it), and felt as if she dreamed, and yet is confident she did not dream. When she was thus gone, she saw two paths. One appeared very broad and crooked and that turned to the left hand; the other appeared strait and very narrow and that went up the hill to the right hand. She travelled, she said, for some time up the narrow right hand path, till at length something seemed to obstruct her journey. She sometimes called it darkness, and then described it otherwise, and seemed to compare it to a block or bar. She then remembered, what she had heard me say about "striving to enter in at the strait gate" (although she took little notice of it, at the time when she heard me discourse upon that subject), and thought she would climb over this bar. But just as she was thinking of this, she came back again, as she termed it, meaning that she came to herself; whereupon her soul was extremely distressed, apprehending she had now turned back and forsaken Christ, and that there was therefore no hope of mercy for her.

As I was sensible that trances and imaginary views of things are of dangerous tendency in religion, when sought after and depended upon; so I could not but be much concerned about this exercise, especially at first; apprehending this might be a design of Satan to bring a blemish upon the work of God here by introducing visionary scenes, imaginary terrors, and all manner of mental disorders and delusions, in the room of genuine convictions of sin, and the enlightening influences of the blessed Spirit. I was almost resolved to declare that I looked upon this to be one of Satan's devices, and to caution my people against it, and the like exercises, as such.

However, I determined first to inquire into her knowledge, to see whether she had any just views of things that might be the occasion of her present distressing concern, or if it was a mere fright arising only from imaginary terrors. I asked her different questions respecting man's primitive, and more especially his present state, and respecting her own heart; which she answered rationally, to my surprise. I thought it was next to impossible, if not altogether so, that a pagan who was become a child through age should in that state gain so much knowledge by any mere human instruction, without being remarkably enlightened by a divine influence.

I then proposed to her the provision made in the gospel for the salvation of sinners, and the ability and willingness of Christ "to save to the uttermost all (old as well as young) that come to him". To which she seemed to give a hearty assent. But instantly replied, "Ay, but I cannot come; my wicked heart will not come to Christ; I do not know how to come." This she spoke in anguish of spirit, striking on her breast, with tears in her eyes, and with such earnestness in her looks as was indeed piteous and affecting. She seems to be really convinced of her sin and her need of a change of heart, and her concern is abiding and constant. So that nothing appears but that this exercise may have a saving issue. Indeed it seems hopeful, seeing she is so solicitous to obtain an interest in Christ that her heart (as she expresses it) prays day and night.

How far God may make use of the imagination in awakening some persons under these, and such like circumstances, I cannot pretend to determine. Or whether this exercise be from a divine influence, I shall leave others to judge. But this I must say, that its effects hitherto bespeak it to be such. For the woman, I am sure, never heard divine things treated of in the manner she now viewed them in; and it would seem strange she should get such a notion of them from the mere working of her own fancy, without some superior aid. Yet I must say, I have looked upon it as one of the glories of this work of grace among the Indians, and a special evidence of its being from a divine influence, that there has, till now, been no appearance of such things, no visionary notions, trances, and imaginations intermixed with those convictions of sin, and solid consolations, that numbers have been made the subject of. And might I have had my desire, there had been no appearance of anything of this nature at all.

December 28th

Discoursed to my people in the catechism method I lately entered upon. In the improvement of my discourse, wherein I was comparing man's present with his primitive state and showing what he had fallen from, and the miseries he is now involved in, and exposed to in his natural estate; and pressing sinners to take a view of their deplorable circumstances without Christ, as also to strive that they might obtain an interest in Him; and the Lord, I trust, granted a remarkable influence of His blessed Spirit to accompany what was spoken, and a great concern appeared in the assembly.

In particular, there were two or three persons who appeared to be brought to the last exercises of a preparatory work and reduced almost to extremity, being in a great measure convinced of the impossibility of their helping themselves or of mending their own hearts. They seemed to be upon the point of giving up all hope in themselves and of venturing upon Christ as naked, helpless, and undone. Yet they were in distress and anguish because they saw no safety in so doing, unless they could do something towards saving themselves. One of these persons was the very aged woman above mentioned, who now appeared "weary and heavy laden" with a sense of her sin and misery and her perishing need of an interest in Christ.

Lord's Day December 29th

Preached from John 3; 1-5. A number of white people were present, as is usual upon the Sabbath. The discourse was accompanied with power, and seemed to have a silent, but deep and piercing influence upon the audience. Many wept and there were some tears among the white people, as well as the Indians. But the impressions made upon their hearts appeared chiefly by the extraordinary earnestness of their attention and their heavy sighs.

After public worship was over, I went to my house, proposing to preach again after a short season of intermission. But they soon came in one after another to know "what they should do to be saved". The divine Spirit in such a manner set home upon their hearts what I spoke to them that the house was soon filled with cries and groans. They all flocked together upon this occasion, and those whom I had reason to think in a Christless state were almost universally seized with concern for their souls.

It was an amazing season of power among them, and seemed as if God had "bowed the heavens, and come down". So astonishingly prevalent was the operation upon old as well as young that it seemed as if none would be left in a secure and natural state. I was ready to think then that I should never again despair of the conversion of any man or woman living, be they who or what they would.

It is impossible to give a just and lively description of the appearance of things at this season, at least such as to convey a bright and adequate idea of the effects of this influence. A number might now be seen rejoicing that God had not taken away the powerful influence of His blessed Spirit from this place. They were refreshed to see so many "striving to enter in at the strait gate" and animated with such concern for them that they wanted "to push them forward", as some of them expressed it.

At the same time numbers both of men and women, old and young, might be seen in tears and some in anguish of spirit, appearing in their very countenances like condemned malefactors bound towards the place of execution, with a heavy solicitude sitting in their faces; so that there seemed here (as I thought) a lively emblem of the solemn day of accounts, a mixture of heaven and hell, of joy and anguish inexpressible. The concern and religious affection was such that I could not pretend to have a service among them; but spent the time in discoursing to one and another, as I thought most proper and seasonable for each, and sometimes addressed them all together, and finally concluded with prayer.

Such were their circumstances at this season that I could scarce have half an hour's rest from speaking from about half an hour before twelve o'clock (at which time I began public worship) till past seven at night. There appeared to be four or five persons newly awakened this day and the evening before, some of whom but very lately came among us.

December 31st

Spent some hours this day in visiting my people from house to house, and conversing with them about their spiritual concerns, endeavouring to press upon Christless souls the necessity of a change of heart. I scarce left a house without leaving some or other of its inhabitants in tears, appearing solicitously engaged to obtain an interest in Christ.

The Indians are now gathered together from all quarters to this place, and have built them little cottages, so that more than twenty families live within a quarter of a mile of me, a very convenient situation in regard both of public and private instruction.

January 2nd 1746

Visited several persons newly come among us who had scarce ever heard anything of Christianity except the name. Endeavoured to instruct them in the first principles of religion, in the most easy and familiar way I could. There are strangers from remote parts almost continually dropping in among us, so that I have occasion repeatedly to open the Word to them in this way.

Lord's Day January 5th

Discoursed this day from Matthew 12;10-13 regarding the man with the withered hand, and the sheep in the pit on the Sabbath. There appeared not so much liveliness in divine service as previously. The same truths that have before produced many tears seemed now to have no influence in any special way. Near night I proposed to follow my usual method of catechizing. But while we were engaged in the first prayer, the power of God seemed to descend on the assembly in such a remarkable manner, and so many appeared under pressing concern for their souls, that I thought it much more expedient to insist upon the plentiful provision made by divine grace for the redemption of perishing sinners, than to ask them questions on points of doctrine.

March 8th

Catechized in the evening. My people answered the questions put to them very well. I can perceive their knowledge of religion increases daily. What is still more desirable, the divine influence that has been so remarkable among them appears to continue in some good measure. So it seemed in the assembly this evening. Some were melted under a sense of the divine goodness and their own barrenness and ingratitude, and hated themselves on this account, as one of them afterwards expressed it.

Lord's Day March 9th

Preached from Luke 10; 38-42 regarding Martha and "the one thing needful". The Word was attended with power and energy, numbers being affected to obtain the one thing needful. Sundry who had given good evidences of being truly gracious were much affected with a sense of the want of their spirituality, and saw the need they stood in of growing in grace.

In the afternoon I sought to follow my course of catechizing, but while we were engaged in the first prayer, in the Indian language (as usual), a great part of the company was so much moved and affected with divine things that I went straight to the most practical truths as I had done on one or more previous occasions. Sundry were so deeply affected by their own barrenness, and their unworthy treatment of the Redeemer, that they looked on Him as pierced by themselves. Some poor awakened sinners were in anguish of souls to obtain a like interest in Christ.

Methinks it would have refreshed the heart of any who truly love Zion's interests to have been in the midst at this time and witnessed the effects upon saints and sinners alike. … Those who had any relish for divine things could not but have cried out, "How amiable are Thy tabernacles, O Lord of Hosts!" After worship was over numbers came into the house where we sang and discoursed of divine things.

One woman, who, if I may venture to say, if I may be allowed to say so much of any person I ever saw, was "filled with joy unspeakable and full of glory", and could not but burst forth in prayer and praises to God before us all, crying sometimes in English and sometimes in Indian: "O, blessed Lord, do come, do come. Oh, do take me away, do let me die and go to Jesus Christ! I am afraid if I live I shall sin again. … Oh, how can I live in this world?" When she had a little recovered she said to me, "I have many times heard you speak of the goodness and sweetness of Christ, that He is better than all the world. But oh! I knew nothing what you meant, I never believed you! I never believed you! But now I know it is true."

Of what is usually called the preparatory work, I scarce ever saw one more bowed down under a conviction of her sin, and as regards what may be called the attendants of the subsequent blessing I scarce ever saw the quiet spirit of resignation given to one whose husband lay at the point of death at the time. Now she could freely trust her all with God for time and eternity. The consequences of this joy are no less desirable and satisfactory since she appears to be of a most tender, broken-hearted, and affectionate disposition, as exemplary in her life and conversation as any person in my congregation. May she grow in grace, and in the knowledge of Christ.

March 15th

My people answered the questions put to them with surprising readiness and judgment. There was some warmth and sense of divine things among those who, I have reason to hope, are real Christians, while I was discoursing upon "peace of conscience, and joy in the Holy Ghost." These seemed quickened and enlivened in divine service, though there was not so much appearance of concern among those I have reason to think in a Christless state.

Lord's Day March 16th

Preached today from Hebrews 2;1-3. Divine truths seemed to have considerable weight upon many of the hearers. The impressions appeared, in general, to be deep and affecting, not superficial, noisy, or affected. Toward night discoursed again upon the great salvation. Numbers wept affectionately, and, to appearance, unfeignedly, so that the Spirit of God seemed to be moving upon the face of the assembly. Baptized the woman mentioned in my *Journal* of last Lord's Day. My house being thronged with people in the evening, I spent the time with them in religious exercises until my nature was almost spent. They are so unwearied and insatiable in their thirsting after Christian knowledge, that I can sometimes scarce avoid labouring so as to greatly exhaust my strength and spirits.

March 19th

Sundry of the persons who went with me to the Forks of Delaware in February last, having been detained there through the illness of one of the company, returned home but this day. Whereupon my people met together of their own accord especially to give thanks to God for His preserving goodness, and recovery to him who had been sick.

Lord's Day March 23rd

There being about fifteen strangers present, some of whom had not been to any religious meeting before, I spoke in a manner suited to their circumstances, from Hosea 13;9, "O Israel, thou hast destroyed thyself." I opened in the plainest manner I could man's apostasy, and ruined state, after having spoken some things respecting the being and perfections of God, and His creation of man in a state of uprightness. In the afternoon endeavoured to open the glorious provision of God for the redemption of sinners by making His own dear Son to suffer for them and satisfy justice on their behalf. There was not the concern I had hoped for, especially among the strangers.

Near sunset I felt an uncommon concern over these and in this frame visited the houses where they were. I continued my discourse with fervency, till we were obliged to remove to the house where we usually meet for public worship. Here I spoke from Luke 19;10. "For the Son of man is come to seek and to save that which was lost"; endeavouring to open up the mercy, compassion and concern of Christ for lost, helpless sinners.

There was much visible concern in the assembly, and I doubt not but what a divine influence accompaned what was spoken to the hearts of many. In particular one very rugged young man, who seemed as if nothing would move him, was now brought to tremble like the jailer. The pagans that were awakened seemed at once to put off their savage roughness, and became orderly and humane in their carriage. When they first came I exhorted my religious people to take pains with them, and instruct them in Christianity but when they attempted something of that nature the strangers would go to other houses to avoid hearing them. Whereupon some of the serious persons agreed to disperse themselves in the several parts of the settlement so that wherever the strangers went they met with some instructive discourse.

But now there was no need of using policy in order to get an opportunity of speaking to them about their spiritual concerns for they were so far touched with a sense of their perishing state, as made them yield to the closest addresses regarding their need for an interest in the great Redeemer.

BIBLIOGRAPHY

The Works of Jonathan Edwards
London
Two volumes
Memoir S.E. Dwight
1865

Jonathan Edwards Iain Murray
Biography
Banner of Truth
1987

Life and Diary of David Brainerd
Moody Press
Edited by Jonathan Edwards
1949

SOME OTHER BOOKS BY THE AUTHOR

In Search of Freedom
The Pilgrim Fathers and New England

Servant of a Covenant God
The life and times of John Warburton

John Gill
The 18th - century theologian

The Reformers Series
Martin Luther
Zwingli and Calvin
John Knox
Wycliffe and Huss

The Martyrs Series
William Tyndale
Thomas Cranmer
The Geneva Exiles
The Marian Martyrs

To Glory in a Blaze
The Martyrs Series in one volume

The Life and Hymns of John Cennick
The 18th - century hymnwriter

Reformation and Counter Reformation
A brief account of attempts to change the Protestant heritage of Britain

Spirit of Truth
Some aspects of charismatic teaching

Obtainable from:

GOSPEL STANDARD TRUST PUBLICATIONS
12(b) Roundwood Lane, Harpenden, Herts.
AL5 3DD, England.